VENI SANCTE SPIRITUS

Spiritus Domini replevit orbem terrarum;
et hoc quod continet omnia, scientiam habet vocis.

The Spirit of the Lord hath filled the whole world;
and that which containeth all things,
hath knowledge of the voice.

—Wisdom 1:7

VENI SANCTE SPIRITUS

The Sequence of the Mass for Pentecost

by

THE REV. NICHOLAUS GIHR, D.D.

translated by

REV. L. M. DOOLEY, S. V. D.

BENEDICTUS BOOKS
Manchester, NH

BENEDICTUS
BOOKS

Veni Sancte Spiritus was first published in 1924 by Herder, Freiburg, and in English in 1947 by the St. Francis Xavier Mission House "Miramar," Island Creek, Massachusetts. The present edition by Benedictus Books® prefers fidelity to the superb translation of 1947 over modernized diction, and so contains only minimal formatting and editorial changes that do not affect the original content or style. Citations have been added or amended where necessary.

Approbations from the original:
Imprimi Potest: Very Rev. Francis Humel, S. V. D., Eastern Provincial, Girard, PA
Nihil obstat: Rt. Rev. Hugh L. Blunt, LL. D., *Censor Librorum*
Imprimatur: Most Rev. Richard J. Cushing, D. D., *Archiepiscopus*
Boston, March 23, 1947

Scripture references follow the Challoner version of the Douay-Rheims Bible, per the imprint of John Murphy (Baltimore, 1899).

Cover by Updatefordesign Studio
Cover Art: *Holy Ghost* (adapted from public domain)
Interior illustration: *Pentecost* from the *Small Passion*
by Albrecht Dürer (ca. 1510), added from the public domain.

Benedictus Books
Box 5284, Manchester, NH 03108
1-800-888-9344

www.PrayBenedictus.com

ISBN 979-8-88911-102-3

eBook ISBN 979-8-88911-103-0

Library of Congress Control Number: 2023950161

First printing

CONTENTS

Scripture Citation Abbreviations

1 Cor	1 Corinthians
1 Esd	1 Esdras (Ezra)
1 Jn	1 John
1 Kgs	1 Kings (1 Samuel)
1 Mc	1 Machabees
1 Par	1 Paralipomenon (1 Chronicles)
1 Pt	1 Peter
1 Thes	1 Thessalonians
1 Tm	1 Timothy
2 Cor	2 Corinthians
2 Esd	2 Esdras (Nehemiah)
2 Jn	2 John
2 Kgs	2 Kings (2 Samuel)
2 Mc	2 Machabees
2 Par	2 Paralipomenon (2 Chronicles)
2 Pt	2 Peter
2 Thes	2 Thessalonians
2 Tm	2 Timothy
3 Jn	3 John
3 Kgs	3 Kings (1 Kings)
4 Kgs	4 Kings (2 Kings)
Abd	Abdias (Obadiah)
Acts	Acts of the Apostles
Agg	Aggeus (Haggai)
Am	Amos
Apoc	Apocalypse (Revelation)
Bar	Baruch
Cant	Canticle of Canticles (Song of Songs)
Col	Colossians
Dn	Daniel
Dt	Deuteronomy
Eccles	Ecclesiastes
Ecclus	Ecclesiasticus (Sirach)
Eph	Ephesians
Est	Esther
Ex	Exodus

Ez	Ezechiel (Ezekiel)
Gal	Galatians
Gn	Genesis
Hb	Habacuc (Habakkuk)
Heb	Hebrews
Is	Isaias (Isaiah)
Jas	James
Jer	Jeremias (Jeremiah)
Jb	Job
Jl	Joel
Jn	John (Gospel)
Jon	Jonas (Jonah)
Jo	Josue (Joshua)
Jude	Jude
Jgs	Judges
Jdt	Judith
Lam	Lamentations
Lv	Leviticus
Lk	Luke
Mal	Malachias (Malachi)
Mk	Mark
Mt	Matthew
Mi	Micheas (Micah)
Na	Nahum
Nm	Numbers
Os	Osee (Hosea)
Phlm	Philemon
Phil	Philippians
Prv	Proverbs
Ps	Psalms
Rom	Romans
Ru	Ruth
Soph	Sophonias (Zephaniah)
Ti	Titus
Tb	Tobias (Tobit)
Ws	Wisdom
Zac	Zacharias (Zechariah)

Publisher's Preface

Msgr. Nicholaus Gihr (1839–1924), a scholar and priest of the Archdiocese of Freiburg, was regarded as one of the most outstanding German liturgists and dogmatic theologians of his time. Contemporary to the great French liturgist Dom Prosper Guéranger, Gihr's monumental work *The Holy Sacrifice of the Mass* (1877) would have similarly far-reaching influence on the theological discourse of several pontificates, including those of Bl. Pius IX, St. Pius X, Benedict XV, and Pius XI.

Following on the success of his book-length meditation on the *Dies Irae*,[1] Gihr's meditation on the *Veni Sancte Spiritus* was first published in Freiburg (Herder: 1924), and exhibits the same degree of expansive scholarship and depth of insight found in his magnum opus, paired with a certain sweetness of prose that well befits the Golden Sequence.

It is worth noting that Gihr comments on each of the ten Sequence stanzas in pairs, for which reason there are ten total stanzas,

1 For the definitive edition of this work in English, see *Dies Irae: The Sequence of the Mass for the Dead* (Manchester: Benedictus Books, 2021).

treated in five different sections that we have sought to render clear through updated formatting. For this new edition, we have also expanded annotations whenever possible, and where any original references were obscure, we have simply reproduced these without alteration. Finally, we have omitted the original translator's epilogue, finding that this added nothing of substantial merit to the work, but rather tended to distract from the meditative character of Msgr. Gihr's work as a whole.

Author's Preface

"It is a common and well-grounded lament that in teaching the Word of God, the doctrine concerning the third Person of the Blessed Trinity is to large extent sadly neglected. As a natural consequence, there is among the generality of Christians very little of either speculative knowledge or practical understanding of the essential significance and importance of the devotion to the Holy Ghost in the economy of Christian belief and practice. There is at best but a minimum appreciation of His fruitful mission in the Church, a relatively faint longing for His immeasurable gifts and graces, and still less realization of the absolute necessity for His light and strength in the soul's interior life. This manifest neglect is closely related to the fact that the proper concept and the right understanding of the supernatural has been almost completely lost sight of in our day. For devout religious living this situation has the direst consequences: in some it occasions overweening pride and Pelagian darkness and obscurity; in others, it leads to discouragement. On the contrary, rightly understood and deeply appreciated and pondered, the doctrine concerning the Holy Ghost and His efficacious activity in transforming the soul is singularly effective in promoting the spirit of prayer and of zeal, as well as humility, conscientious fidelity to God, and courageous perseverance."[1]

Other spiritual writers are of the same opinion. These considerations justify every effort to further the devotion to the Holy Spirit among the clergy and the laity by a thoroughgoing explanation of the exceedingly meritorious Pentecost Sequence.

More than anyone else should the priest be a zealous adorer of the Holy Ghost, since, by virtue of his sacred calling, he stands in a particularly intimate relationship with the Holy Spirit. The third Person of the Blessed Trinity is Creator or Preserver, and Perfecter of the supernatural life in redeemed mankind; through His mystical divine governance, He sanctifies and rules the entire Mystical Body of Christ—the Church. As the Source and Dispenser of all graces, the Holy Ghost establishes and perfects the higher life in the redeemed, whereby He affects souls not only in an invisible and immediate manner, but makes special use of visible means and instruments. Among these, the priesthood and the liturgy have a superior place; through both, the Holy Ghost dispenses the graces of redemption in the greatest profusion.

In the discharge of his sacred ministry, the priest is, therefore, not only the servant of Christ and the Church, but also the organ of the Holy Spirit, Who sanctifies souls chiefly through the liturgical functions (sacrifice, Sacraments, sacramentals), the accomplishment of which is entrusted to the priesthood. The Holy Ghost dispenses the sacerdotal power. He creates the priests, and ordains them "as pastors and teachers for the perfecting of the saints, for the work of the ministry, for the edifying of the Body of Christ" (Eph 4:11–12). As if imparting charismatic gifts, He furnishes the ordained with the riches of sanctifying grace, and thereby makes them capable of "dispensing the mysteries of God" (1 Cor 4:1) in a worthy, admirable, and fruitful manner, as well as with fidelity and prudence. The Holy Ghost grants to the sacerdotal labors all blessings, all success and favorable results; for, to "give the increase" (1 Cor 3:6) "surpasses not only the lowliness of man, but also the sublimity of the angels, and proceeds exclusively from the Holy Ghost, i.e., the most Holy Trinity."[2]

Since therefore the life and labors of the priest belong wholly to the sphere of Faith and to the kingdom of grace, he is entirely dependent upon the Holy Ghost, and step-by-step in need of His supernatural assistance. In order to fulfill his sublime calling worthily (see Eph 4:1), and to carry on his sacred ministry so as to merit the blessing of God, he must be replenished with the Holy Ghost (*repletus Spiritu Sancto*—Acts 4:8) and be full of the Holy Ghost (*plenus Spiritu Sancto*—Acts 11:24), and in all his actions be led and moved by the Spirit of God (see Gal 5:18; and Rom 8:14), that is, by a prompt, resolute obedience to the light and the inspirations of the Holy Ghost, he must lead a truly spiritual life. This supernatural living, working, suffering, and praying in the Holy Spirit (see 1 Cor 12:2ff.) presupposes humble submission to the authority of the Holy Ghost, as well as perfect union and constant intimacy with the Holy Spirit, that is, tendering profound homage to the third Person of the Blessed Trinity, by adoring Him in the spirit of faith, invoking Him with unbounded trust, and offering Him heartfelt gratitude and love.

Accordingly, a more than ordinary fervor and zeal in fostering a genuine devotion to the Holy Ghost is as necessary as it is excellent for the priest of God that he may become an ecclesiastic in the truest sense of the word, and carry on his august mission as a genuine priest, that is, so that he may excite in others a tendency toward a deeply spiritual life, and spare no pains to foster and perfect it.

A spiritual man, a religious in the true sense of the term (*homo spiritualis*), is the priest alone who takes a determined stand against the assaults of the fleshly, worldly, and materialistic spirit, that he may at all times and everywhere live, act, and think in the spirit of Jesus Christ.

Like the apostles, like all apostolic men, the priest received in the Sacrament of holy orders, not the spirit of this world (*spiritum hujus mundi*), but the Spirit that is of God (*Spiritum, qui ex Deo est*), that he might know the gifts bestowed upon him by God, and show his gratitude by the use and realization of these gifts. For true priestly life and activity, constant furtherance of devotion to the Holy Ghost should be perseveringly practiced every day. Filled with longing, the priestly heart and mouth should be opened to draw down the Holy Spirit and, as it were, to absorb Him (cf. Ps 118:131), as one inhales the air; that is, in all the duties of his state (Holy Mass, recitation of the breviary, dispensing the Sacraments, preaching, catechizing, visiting the sick), as well as in his practices of private devotion (meditation, spiritual reading, examen of conscience, visits to the Blessed Sacrament, the Rosary, the Stations of the Cross, study), even if they be of only short duration, he should earnestly implore the light and strength of the Holy Spirit.

"If he prays, he will be enlightened; if he calls upon God, the Spirit of Wisdom will come to him" (see Ws 7:7). Wherever the Holy Spirit is invoked and honored in the spirit of humility and devotion, wherever His powerful grace rules and governs, there heart and soul are newly created (see Ps 103:30); there the sweet, precious, and blessed fruits of the supernatural life flourish and yield bountiful returns: "Charity, joy, peace, patience, benignity, goodness, longanimity, mildness, faith, modesty, continency, chastity" (Gal 5:22–23).

Many saints were distinguished for their ardent devotion to the Holy Ghost. The seraphic virgin Teresa began nearly all her letters with the pious wish and blessing: "May the Holy Spirit (or the grace of the Holy Ghost) be with you at all times." Thus she wrote from the fullness of her heart. As she relates in her autobiography,[3] she received a grace on Pentecost that she herself considered one of the greatest, because of the many and signal favors which it imparted to her soul. On the eve of this feast, she had retired to a quiet place, and there read a treatise on Pentecost. But while she was meditating on what she had read, she was seized with a powerful ecstasy. Above her head she saw a large, bright dove, and heard the rustle of its wings. Heavenly peace filled her soul; during the greater part of the feast, she was in rapture, and all her exterior senses seemed as if bound; she was almost prostrate under the weight of this extraordinary grace, and felt herself so deeply immersed in the superabundance of interior joy, that she saw and heard scarcely anything further. Since that day she felt greatly strengthened in virtue; and her heart was more than ordinarily inflamed with ardent love of God.

A very exceptional instance of devotion to the Holy Ghost is shown us in the life of Blessed Crescentia Kaufbeuren, who lived in the eighteenth century. This child of grace gave early evidence of the operations of the Holy Spirit in her soul; she felt herself drawn to adore Him in the spirit of living faith and intense love. She would be a pure temple of the Holy Ghost; and she was, therefore, resolved not only to free her heart of the slightest stains of imperfection, but also to adorn it with every virtue. In all difficulties, temptations, and sufferings, she at once called upon the Holy Ghost. She prepared herself for the feast of Pentecost through a fervent novena, during which she devoted herself to severe penances, frequent meditations, ceaseless prayer, and aspirations of love. She took delight in repeating often the *Veni Creator Spititus* and other hymns of the Church. On the great feast itself and during the octave, she was consequently favored with a generous share of the gifts of the Holy Ghost and extraordinary proofs of grace. This heartfelt interior familiarity with the Holy Spirit was signalized by numerous visions. During one of these raptures, she once heard the words: "Him who loves nothing but Me alone, I will fortify with My grace." An extraordinary measure of divine grace was accorded her on this occasion, flooding her soul with a wholly new light. This light was a rare, exceedingly valuable benefit to her, for it disclosed the depths of her nothingness and all merely natural movements with the clearness of the midday sun, at the same time enabling her to observe and realize distinctly the promptings and workings of grace in her innermost soul.[4]

The time from Christ's Ascension to Trinity Sunday is particularly opportune for renewing our fervor and zeal in venerating and invoking the Holy Spirit, each year as the holy season rolls around. Pentecost constitutes the centerpiece as well as the climax of this season, which partly serves as a preparation (novena) for the Coming of the Holy Ghost, and partly as a subsequent celebration of the mysteries of the feast.

Pentecost is one of the most prominent feasts, and its origin dates to apostolic time. St. Augustine numbers "the annual celebration of the Passion, the Resurrection, and Ascension of our Lord, as well as the Descent of the Holy Ghost" among the traditions that are observed throughout the world.[5] "Pentecost is hallowed through the Coming of the Holy Ghost, and is immediately connected with Easter; for it is always directed toward that day which is made glorious by the Resurrection of Christ."[6] As in point of time, so also in rank, Pentecost follows Easter; both feasts are celebrated liturgically in almost the same manner.

Pentecost is rightly considered the feast of the Holy Ghost. The circumstance of the celebration is first of all a fact of the past; the extraordinary manifestation and visible Descent of the Holy

Ghost upon the disciples assembled in the upper chamber, i.e., the newly founded Church of Christ. Conjointly with this fact, a mystery is commemorated that belongs to the present, since it is always repeated and ever continues: the abiding, invisible effusion of the Holy Ghost upon the Church and all the faithful. As was the case nineteen centuries ago, so even today the Holy Ghost is still sent to the faithful. This circumstance bestows upon the feast of Pentecost a peculiar character and endows it particularly with a lofty, practical significance. Just as the light and warmth of day comes to the earth and every creature upon it from the sun, so the light of truth and the warmth of the grace of Jesus Christ streams down upon the whole Church and all her members, emanating from the Holy Ghost as fountainhead and source.

It is the Holy Ghost Who teaches pope and bishops all truth and reminds them of all the words of Christ. It is the Holy Ghost Who awakens and sustains in the faithful the susceptibility and the understanding for the teaching of the Church. The Holy Ghost grants to the Catholic priesthood the divine power to fulfill the eternal sacrifice of the New Law, and to dispense the Sacraments of salvation. The Holy Ghost grants to souls sanctifying grace and all actual graces, which yield a bountiful fruitage of Christian living and genuine virtue. It is the Holy Ghost Who thunders and lightens in the word of God; Who drops into the souls of the just the gentle rains and dews of heaven, for the conversion from sin, and for growth in holiness without end.

All who belong to the Church have received the Holy Ghost, and in manifold ways experience His merciful efficacy.[7] Thus the Holy Ghost completes and crowns the work of redemption, renewing the face of the earth through the Church and in the Church (see Ps 103:30). Therefore, "let the entire earth rejoice with overflowing joy" at the Coming of the Holy Ghost; therefore Pentecost is such a great and glorious feast of rejoicing, extolled by the Fathers with words of enthusiastic praise.

Every Catholic knows full well that Pentecost must be solemnized as one of the most sublime of all feasts; and there can be no shadow of doubt about the veneration that is due to this feast, which has been sanctified by the Holy Ghost in so wonderful a manner by the fullness of His gifts. Let us all be zealous in the devout commemoration of the feast of Pentecost, worshipping the Holy Spirit with heartfelt jubilation—this Spirit Who sanctifies the entire Catholic Church and fills every soul, Who infuses faith (*inspirator fidei*) and teaches knowledge (*doctor scientiae*), Who is the Source of love (*fons dilectionis*), the Seal of chastity (*signaculum castitatis*), and the Fount of every virtue (*totius causa virtutis*).

The hearts of the faithful should rejoice that, throughout the world, the one God, Father, Son, and Holy Ghost, is extolled and acknowledged by all tongues, and that in efficacy and gifts of grace, that mystery continues which was symbolized by the appearance of tongues of fire. For the Spirit of Truth Himself causes the dwelling of His glory to be irradiated by the diffusion of His light, and tolerates neither darkness nor tepidity in His temple (*in templo suo nec tenebrosum aliquid vult esse nec tepidum*).

Pentecost is held in highest esteem and veneration the world over, since it was hallowed fifty days after the Resurrection of the Lord by the promised and expected Descent of the Holy Ghost upon the apostles and a multitude of the faithful. The Holy Ghost came, not to take up His dwelling for the first time in the hearts of the faithful (*non, ut tunc primum esse sanctorum habitator inciperet*), but to inflame the souls consecrated to Him with more ardent love, and inundate them with a greater fullness of grace (*sed ut sacrata sibi pectora et ferventius accenderet et copiosius inundaret*); therefore He did not then begin to distribute His gifts, but only dispensed them in more generous measure; He did not then begin His efficacious activity, because He distributed His riches more abundantly (*nec ideo novus opere, quia ditior largitate*).[8]

Chrysostom perceives in the Coming of the Holy Ghost and His gifts a clear "proof" as well as a "pledge of our reconciliation with God," and, in his second homily on Pentecost, he gives enthusiastic expression to the exalted sentiments that filled his heart: "God has dispensed to us today great and glorious gifts that surpass all human eloquence. Let us, therefore, rejoice together; let us exult and magnify the Lord; for this day is a feast day on which we assemble with heartfelt joy in the house of God.... Not long ago, we celebrated the feast of the Cross and the Passion, the feast of the Resurrection, and then the Ascension of our Lord Jesus Christ; today we have arrived at the crown of all Goodness, and at the 'metropolis of feasts,' and have received the fruits of the promises of the Lord.... Today He favors us with the Coming of the Holy Ghost, and, through Him, dispenses countless blessings from heaven. For tell me, has not everything that is conducive to the salvation of our souls been imparted to us by the Holy Ghost?... Everything with which the Church of God is adorned flows to us from this Fountain."

So lofty, so sublime, and so rich in grace is this feast of Pentecost for all who open their hearts and, as it were, inhale the Holy Spirit with breathings of desire, that it beggars description. A novena should prepare our hearts and make them susceptible of ever-greater intimacy with the Holy Ghost and participation in His gifts; then the feast with its octave will truly be a time of salvation, more particularly since we so often address to heaven the humble, trustful, and sincere petitions of the Sequence.

Brevity and compactness joined with inexhaustible content, pleasing simplicity, and transparency with depth of thought, and vivacity of sentiment, appropriate figures of speech with surprising analogies and antitheses—these are the excellences our Pentecostal Hymn portrays, ranking it among the most fragrant blossoms in the garden of holy poesy. There is perfect harmony between its attractive content and the melodious sweetness of language in which it is expressed. The activity of the Holy Ghost in the souls of the faithful is here preeminently envisioned in His capacity as our "Helper" and "Comforter" in sorrow and strife, in danger and death. But this strain always seizes mightily upon the inner strings of the restless, tormented human heart, and therefore finds here its truest and most natural expression, in calling from the "abyss" of its poverty and misery unto the abyss of divine compassion. (*Abyssus abyssum invocat*—Ps 41:8). This explains the peculiar character of the Pentecost Sequence, which contains neither a delineation of supernatural facts, nor formal praises, but only humble invocations to the Holy Ghost.

From beginning to end, it is a prayer of supplication, the petitions of which are so heartfelt and interior, that one easily perceives in them the heavenly breathings of the Holy Ghost, Who Himself pleads for us with unspeakable groanings (see Rom 8:26). At the same time, these petitions are so comprehensive that they may be suggested to all the faithful; for they express with a natural, lively feeling, the needs of the soul in the various stages and changing moods of the spiritual life. Thus the Sequence lays a distinguished claim to popularity, in the noblest sense of the term.

—*The Author*

ENDNOTES

1 Jungmann, S. J., *Theorie der geistlichen Beredsamkeit*, 400–402.
2 Augustine, *Tractates on the Gospel of John*, Tractate 80, no. 2.
3 See chap. 38.
4 See Ignatius Jeiler, O. S. F., *Life of Blessed Crescentia of Kaufbeuren*.
5 See Letter 54 to Januarius, chap. 1.
6 Leo the Great, Letter to All the Bishops of Sicily, chap. 3.
7 See Laurent.
8 See Leo the Great, Sermon 77.

VENI SANCTE SPIRITUS

I

Introduction by the Translator

On May 4, 1897, His Holiness, Pope Leo XIII, of glorious memory, addressed an encyclical on the Holy Spirit, *Divinum Illud*, to the Catholic world. In its introduction, he briefly alluded to the two chief ends of his long pontificate, which comprised the restoration of the principles of Christian life, both in rulers and people; and secondly, the promotion of the reunion of those who had fallen away from the Catholic Church either through heresy or through schism. He continues: "But now that We are looking forward to the approach of the closing days of Our life, Our soul is deeply moved to dedicate to the Holy Ghost, Who is the life-giving Love, all the work We have done during Our pontificate, that He may bring it to maturity and fruitfulness. In order the better and more fully to carry out this, Our intention, We have resolved to address you at the approaching sacred season of Pentecost concerning the indwelling and miraculous power of the Holy Ghost; and of the extent and efficiency of His action, both in the whole body of the Church and in the individual souls of its members, through the glorious abundance of His divine graces."

Then there followed the dogmatic teaching of the Church concerning the activity of the Holy Spirit in the mystery of the Incarnation, in the Mystic Body of Christ, the Church, and in the souls of the just.

Quite appropriately, therefore, the Holy Father continued: "These sublime truths, which so clearly show forth the infinite goodness of the Holy Ghost toward us, certainly demand that we should direct towards Him the highest homage of our love and devotion. Christians may do this most effectually if they will daily strive to know Him, to love Him, and to implore Him more earnestly; for which reason may this Our exhortation, flowing spontaneously from a paternal heart, reach their ears.... There are certainly many who are very deficient in their knowledge of Him. Yes, they frequently use His name in their religious practices, but their faith is involved in much darkness. Wherefore all preachers and those having care of souls should remember that it it is their duty to instruct their people more diligently and more fully about the Holy Ghost.... What should be chiefly dwelt upon and clearly explained is the multitude and greatness of the benefits which have been bestowed, and are constantly being bestowed, upon us by this Divine Giver, so that errors and ignorance concerning matters of such moment may be entirely dispelled, as unworthy of 'the children of light.' We urge this, not only because it affects a mystery which directly guides us to eternal life, and which must therefore be firmly believed, but also because the more clearly and fully the good is known the more earnestly it is loved." In solemn utterance, the Holy Father then continued: "Wherefore, We decree and command that throughout the whole Catholic Church, this year and in every subsequent year, a Novena shall take place before Whit-Sunday, in all parish churches, and also, if the local Ordinaries think fit, in other churches and oratories." May this book, in English dress, further the ardent wish of the Holy Father that the faithful "daily strive to know Him, to love Him, and to implore Him more earnestly."

And now a passing remark on the word *sequence*. The Sequences were originally so called from the fact that they were a following out in word of the melody of the Alleluia, hence *sequence* from the Latin verb *sequi*, meaning "to follow." "This, however, is not true of the Sequences which survive in the present Roman Missal."[1] The Sequences as such originated toward the end of the ninth century. Today, in our Roman Missal, they are five in number, though up to its revision by Pope St. Pius V in 1570, they were especially numerous. Easter has its *Victimae Paschali Laudes*; Pentecost, its *Veni, Sancte Spiritus*; Corpus Christi, its *Lauda Sion*; the Requiem Mass its *Dies Irae*;[2] and the fifth and last, which was added after the liturgical reform following the Council of Trent, is the *Stabat Mater* for the two feasts commemorating the Dolors of Mary: the one celebrated on the Friday following Passion Sunday, the other on September 15.

The peak of their poetic grandeur was reached by Adam of St. Victor (d. 1192). He is supposed to be the author of the beautiful Sequence, the *Veni, Sancte Spiritus*, called in medieval times the "Golden Sequence." The authorship, however, is still unsettled. It is ascribed to the following: Herman the Cripple (Contractus, d. 1054), the French king Robert (d. 1031), Pope Innocent III (d. 1216), and Stephen Langton, archbishop of Canterbury (d. 1228). However, be that as it may, whoever it was, and here we quote the illustrious Dr. Nicholas Gihr whose elucidation of this Sequence we are about to enjoy: "The Sequence for Whitsunday can have come but from a heart wholly inflamed with the fire of the Holy Ghost. It is an incomparable hymn, breathing of the sweetness of paradise, and regaling us with heaven's sweetest fragrance. Only the soul buried in deep recollection can suspect and taste the wealth of deep thought and affections this Pentecost hymn contains, and that, too, in a form remarkable as much for beauty as for brevity."[3]

The practical question is therefore: Do we need the Holy Spirit Whose exalted powers and effects are so poetically lauded in this Sequence of such rare beauty and loveliness? Definitely yes. We all, without exception, need the uplifting efficacy of the great Vivifier, lest our lives savor of mediocrity and become too ordinary.

For many a soul, the name of the Holy Spirit may sound like the accents of a foreign tongue. Perhaps even today there are many souls who if asked, as were those of old by St. Paul, whether they had received the Holy Spirit, might stammer in like manner: "We have not so much as heard whether there be a Holy Ghost" (Acts 19:2). This seems hardly credible and yet certainly many exist today to whom the Holy Spirit, to say the least, is the "forgotten God." To aver this of our generation, or more pointedly, to have to acknowledge that this is our case, individually, is a poor commentary upon one's spirituality, upon one's religious life. It simply means that, in the concrete, our life externally shows forth no evidence of the inner operations of the soul's sweet Guest. It is a clear indication that our mode of life is very paganistic and at a low pulse of spiritual efficiency.

Now since man's goal is wholly supernatural, it is clear that the propelling power, the activating principle of operation, the motive force, must be supernatural. That dynamo or force is none other than God the Holy Spirit. Hence, when your spiritual motor performs perversely, as it were, in the traffic of life on the great Broadways and Main Streets in your journey toward eternity, and threatens by its inefficiency and faulty mechanism, not only to catapult you ungracefully into the hands of an angry God, but to drag down with you into perdition other hapless souls, it is the Holy Spirit of Whom you stand in need. It is He Who can and will help you adjust your faulty soul-engine and attune it in perfect rhythm and tempo to the requirements and standards of a heavenly mechanism.

And when your archenemy, the wily deceiver of God's children, would tempt you into selling Christ short, bartering your birthright and your nobility as a son or daughter of God, for sinful filthiness that knows not the radiance of God's purity—oh, then, it is the Holy Spirit of Whom you stand in need. As He once brooded over inert matter, hovered over chaos and disorder rampant at the dawn of the earth's history, and wrought beauty and design and order out of that confusion and disorder, so He too will generate a like activity in the confused disorder of your soul, and, by His omnipotent power, will make of you a new creature and a new creation (see 2 Cor 5:17). By the commission of a mortal sin, we demolish hallowed halls of learning, wreck consecrated buildings of worship, blast cherished works of art, and devastate cathedrals of long standing. Now that hallowed hall of learning from which the omniscient God directs the paths of the hurricane, pilots the orbs overhead, arranges the pageantry of the seasons, and guides hearts to sanctification is none other than the lovely chamber of your soul. That consecrated building of worship whence God's angels are constantly coming and going, unceasingly chanting their eternal canticle of "Holy, Holy, Holy" to your sweet and intimate Guest, is none other than your soul in grace. That cherished work of art on which the Holy Spirit has expended the loving ingenuity of His eternal plans, and which is therefore rightly a masterpiece, is none other than your immortal soul. That cathedral upon whose embellishment the very mind of God has deigned to focus the beams of its intelligence, is again none other than your soul of imperishable worth. When man, in a burst of mad fury, ruthlessly lets fall into this storehouse and treasure trove and masterpiece, the bomb of mortal sin, he thereby blasts its beauty and architecture and shatters to utter ruin its lovely lines, that once drew down from the highest heavens the very Godhead, attracted by its priceless beauty and regal, sumptuous splendor. When man does that, it is the Holy Spirit of Whom he stands in need. It is the Holy Spirit alone Who, out of that pitiful wreckage and debris, can reconstruct once more from the blueprints of His eternal mind, a temple fitted worthily to house Him Who "inhabiteth light inaccessible" (1 Tm 6:16).

When you deliberately close your ears to the message of God, willfully set your face against the wholesome pronouncements of God's Vicar upon earth, doggedly refuse to hearken to your pastor's warnings, and blindly elect to go your own willful way, it is the Holy Spirit of Whom you stand in need. He it is Who will assist your human cooperation in rewiring yourself again to the Powerhouse of God, so that your soul may be no longer plunged in Stygian darkness. He will readjust the delicate antennae of your soul, so rudely torn by sin from their receiving set, so that you will again be able and qualified to pick up the never-ending messages of salvation constantly sent out over a worldwide hookup from the Radio City of God's Eternal Broadcasting System. These tidings of the Holy Spirit are His actual graces, His inspirations to do good and to avoid evil, His impulses to embrace and lead, and continue, the life of grace.

When you go into a spiritual slump, when you allow the spirit of lukewarmness and indifference to paralyze your soul's activities, when you permit the fifth columnists to hold anarchistic meetings in your soul's citadel, when you close down your plant due to the Red elements of rebellion and insubordination, then it is the Holy Spirit of Whom you stand in need. He it is Who will step up your spiritual productivity, Who will call off the eternal warring factions, settle the compromising strikers by applying the ethics of Jesus Christ and hoist again over your spiritual workshop the red, white, and blue flag of eternal standards.

It is the Holy Spirit Who will lend the buoyancy and elasticity of youth to your lagging footsteps, so that "if until now you have been remiss in your duties toward the Church, from now on you must be fervent; if until now you have been heedless, from now on you must be watchful; if until now too self-indulgent, from now on you must be guarded; if until now you have been open to censure, from now on you must be without reproach."[4]

It is the Holy Spirit that this weary world needs so sorely to bring it forth to a new creation as of yore, and to arouse it from its languor, from its insipidity, from its stagnant state of lukewarmness, from its sickly swoon of religious inertia and torpor which gradually yields to the fateful sleep of death itself.

The world so complacently wrapped round and enswathed in the sheep's clothing of ravening wolves, enfolded in the silken furs of a clawing impurity, indifferentism, and atheism, stands in sore need of the dazzling lightning flash of the Holy Spirit to purify its foulness, to strike off by a divine suddenness this paralyzing vesture of sin, and to charge the air with the fresh, invigorating, and refreshing ozone of a heavenly atmosphere.

It is His breath we stand in need of which, like a divine aura of sweetness, will gently blow over our barren soul and then the miracle: lilies of purity, roses of love, violets of humility, and flowers of varied hue and pleasing fragrance will spring up to delight the divine Gardener, to make the desert bloom (see Is 35:1) and the fallow land productive, to spread everywhere the "odor of Christ" (2 Cor 2:15).

If with Hamlet[5] you feel that "the time is out of joint," that perfidy and dishonesty have reached a new high, that you are losing faith in human nature, that intrigue and base conduct are sapping the vitals of the nations, that Communism and irreligion are on the increase, that your faith and trust in Divine Providence and in that loving Presence that presides so majestically over the world's destinies, are being slowly but surely undermined, then it is the Holy Spirit of Whom you stand in need. He it is Who will again vivify your drooping spirit, Who will let fall the scales from your failing sight, and permit you to see behind all these changing scenes and confusing moves, the ever-guiding, protecting hand of God, busily active at the shuttles as He holds before Him the strands of nations, weaving unconsciously their own woof—as they will. Peace and calm and confidence will be born afresh if you yield yourselves, childlike, to the sweet, yet powerful, breathings of the Holy Spirit, and remember the immortal lines of Browning: "God's in His heaven, all's right with the world."

If, as an aspirant to the priesthood or religious state, or actively engaged in this sublime walk of life, you begin to weaken in your high resolve; if your lofty aspirations and noble yearnings for the higher things of the spirit begin to wane, if your ardor is being chilled by the sheen and glitter of the intriguing, deceptive world, then it is the Holy Spirit of Whom you stand in need. He, by His sterling gift of fortitude, will give stability to your tortured, vacillating soul and will steady your quailing spirit with the firmness of finely-tempered steel.

It is the Holy Spirit Who will restore to you all "your childhood's chivalries, all your delightful schemings, all your youthful cravings, all your fondest hopes, all your loftiest ideals." He will infuse into your cowardly soul a manly, expansive, throbbing love of Jesus, so that in the words of the saintly, devout Fr. William

Doyle, S.J., "sin would become an impossibility, sacrifice a pleasure and a joy, virtue the longing of every soul."

It is the Holy Spirit Who will gently inspire you with a tender, deep, and holy love of Mary, purest of the pure, and loveliest creature of God's creative hand, and His own Immaculate Spouse.

It is the Holy Spirit Who will make us live our faith wide-awake, Who will make us appreciate the beauty and solidity of its dogmas, the scope of its pronouncements, the grandeur of its Sacraments, the potency of its grace, the privilege of its prayer, the beauty of the Mystical Body, and the entrancing loveliness of His own indwelling.

It is the Holy Spirit Who will teach us to remember the words of St. Leo: "Christian soul, acknowledge thy dignity and having been elevated to a grandeur so sublime, revert not to conduct vile and degenerate."[6]

May the devout, thoughtful, and intelligent perusal of this treatise on the Holy Spirit bring your soul prostrate before Him in adoration. May it show you your spiritual possibilities, and force from you the confession: "O, handful of dust, remember that thou art splendor."

May there ever resound in the fleshly tabernacle of your being, His temple, the song of prayer and the canticle of love, and the *sanctus* bell of a constant devotion, adding zest to the newfound joy of life, increasing your spiritual productive capacity, remobilizing your hitherto spent energies, banishing forever the spirit of coldness to give way to the spirit of fervor in a new burst of happiness. All these actions the Holy Spirit is waiting to inaugurate. Devotion to Him touches off the mighty dynamo that releases these magnificent and fascinating powers. Make your very own the sentiments that filled the devout heart of St. Augustine when he pleaded with the Dispenser of all graces and the Vivifier of all hearts:

Breathe in me, O Holy Spirit,
That my thoughts may all be holy;
Act in me, O Holy Spirit,
That my work, too, may be holy;
Draw my heart, O Holy Spirit,
That I love but what is holy;
Strengthen me, O Holy Spirit,
To defend all that is holy;
Guard me, then, O Holy Spirit,
That I always may be holy.

A heartfelt word of personal appreciation to Sr. Mary Aloysi Kiener, S. N. D., for the value of her scholarship in checking the faithfulness of the translation.

–Fr. Dooley, S. V. D.

ENDNOTES

1 Zundel.
2 Editor's Note: The author of the present work composed a superb book of meditation on the *Dies Irae* as well; see the definitive English edition available from Benedictus Books, 2021.
3 *The Holy Sacrifice of the Mass*, 464.
4 Instruction of the bishop to the ordinands of the subdiaconate.
5 See act 1, scene 5.
6 From a Christmas sermon of Leo the Great; Sermon 21, chap. 3.

II

Text of the Sequence, with English Translation

1
Veni, Sancte Spiritus
Et emitte caelitus
Lucis tuae radium.

Come, Thou holy Paraclete,
And from Thy celestial seat
Send Thy light and brilliancy.

2
Veni, pater pauperum,
Veni, dator munerum,
Veni, lumen cordium.

Father of the poor, draw near
Giver of all gifts, be here,
Come, the soul's true radiancy.

3
Consolator optime,
Dulcis hospes animae,
Dulce refrigerium.

Come, of comforters the best,
Of the soul the sweetest guest,
Come in toil refreshingly.

4
In labore requies,
In aestu temperies,
In fletu solatium.

Thou in labor rest most sweet.
Thou art shadow from the heat,
Comfort in adversity.

5

O lux beatissima,	O Thou light, most pure and blest,
Reple cordis intima,	Shine within the inmost breast
Tuorum fidelium.	Of Thy faithful company.

6

Sine tuo numine	Where Thou art not, man hath naught;
Nihil est in homine,	Ev'ry holy deed and thought
Nihil est innoxium.	Comes from Thy divinity.

7

Lava quod est sordidum,	What is soiled, make Thou pure;
Riga quod est aridum,	What is wounded, work its cure;
Sana quod est saucium.	What is parched, fructify.

8

Flecte quod est rigidum,	What is rigid, gently bend;
Fove quod est frigidum,	What is frozen, warmly tend;
Rege quod est devium.	Strengthen what goes erringly.

9

Da tuis fidelibus,	Fill Thy faithful, who confide
In te confidentibus,	In Thy power to guard and guide,
Sacrum septenarium.	With Thy sevenfold mystery.

10

Da virtutis meritum,	Here Thy grace and mercy send;
Da salutis exitum,	Grant salvation in the end,
Da perenne gaudium.	And in heaven felicity.
Amen.	Amen.

Translation by J. M. Neale

Editor's Note: Although no longer in force, the author originally included mention of the following indulgences for reciting this Sequence: 1) five years; 2) plenary under usual conditions to all who devoutly recite it daily for an entire month. See *The Raccolta*, no. 261.

III

Interpretation

First Stanza (Literal Translation)

Come Holy Spirit, and send forth from
heaven the ray of Thy light.
Come, Father of the poor; come, Giver of gifts;
Come, Light of hearts.

Our prayers to the Holy Spirit should be charged with invincible trust and perfect confidence.

He, Himself, in fact, by the sweet and precious blessings of His grace, anticipates our approach (see Ps 20:4), and, by His awakening and encouraging help, prompts our heart to ask with unspeakable sighs and childlike pleading. But we should ever be mindful that these petitions will be the more speedily and more richly answered in proportion to the more solicitous care we employ in keeping our soul sensitively attuned for the reception of these gifts and favors of the supernatural order. Purity and adornment must characterize the abode where the divine Guest with His retinue of heavenly gifts is to dwell and to hold court.

Such a preparation of heart (see Ps 9:38) is ours by turning away from worldly pursuits, through interior and exterior quiet of soul, through a strict custody of the senses, through recollection of mind and will, and, finally, through penance and compunction of heart and a persevering zeal in prayer.

Such a soul thus artistically adorned commands the ear of the Lord Who "hath heard the desire of the poor" (Ps 9:38). Intense yearning and ardent longing are above all things in demand and are especially effective if one is to attract the Holy Spirit and His gifts.

Through the hundreds of years before Christ's coming, God sought to keep alive and to intensify in the bosom of fallen man, the cherished expectation of a heavenly Savior and Redeemer.

All the agonizing yearning of pre-Christian times is caught up in the Church's liturgy of Advent, above all in the seven Great Antiphons or O-antiphons; nor is their gripping cry of *Veni* stilled until the Expected of the Nations is born of the Blessed Virgin.

After the Savior's Ascension, He still deferred the sending of the Holy Spirit for ten more days.

In the meantime, the flaming desire for the promised "Consoler," for the "Spirit of Truth," for the "Power from on High," was to mount to ever greater and greater intensity in the hearts of the apostles.

Our spirit, likewise, will soar aloft with heavenly desire if, on the one hand, we are keenly alive to our own want, our own misery, our dire need, and, on the other hand, clearly recognize the riches, the surpassing wealth, and the enduring treasures of the Holy Spirit. A searching gaze at our inner self, and a devout glance directed heavenward, impels to this necessary and wholesome knowledge, and consequently, to prayer for the coming of the Holy Spirit.

Because he was "a man of desires," Daniel, the prophet (Dn 9:23), was accorded a revelation concerning Christ, for He fills with the good things of His grace "those hungering after the salvation of God" (see Lk 1:53).

This longing of the heart expresses itself in prayer and in oft-repeated supplication which in turn heightens the yearning desire.

This is the case in the first petition:

Veni, Sancte Spiritus
(Come, Holy Spirit)

The invocation *Veni* (Come) possesses a content at once rich and mysterious so that repetition affords ever greater nourishment to one's heart and spirit.

The Holy Spirit is not alone in His coming to dwell in the souls of the children of men, but with Him we have the entire Trinity.

This truth is announced by the mouth of Our Lord Himself: "If any one love Me, he will keep My word. And My Father will love him and We will come to him and will make Our abode with him" (Jn 14:23).[1] The abiding of the Holy Spirit in the souls of the just is a mystery of faith both deep and consoling; it embraces not the order of nature but the realm of grace. This type of indwelling must be clearly distinguished from that other presence of God in all places and in all things which simply follows as a necessary consequence of His immensity.

Apart from this presence of God in all creatures, there is a very special and exalted mode of presence in the souls of the just.

This special and supernatural presence of God, proceeding from the free will of God, is entitled the "indwelling" and is inseparably associated with sanctifying grace.

Under this aspect, the Holy Spirit abides only in the souls of the just, but, be it understood, in the souls of all the just.

Grace, then, is the celestial tie binding the soul to the Holy Spirit in most intimate union.

It (grace) is the costly adornment consecrating the soul as a worthy dwelling place of the Holy Spirit.

At the same time, it (grace) must be looked upon as a gift and an effect accomplished by the indwelling Spirit. "The charity of God is poured forth in our hearts, by the Holy Spirit Who is given to us" (Rom 5:5).

Naturally the coming of the Holy Spirit (as far as His first indwelling is concerned) coincides with His infusion of sanctifying grace, but, from our viewpoint, it is placed prior in time.

Our sanctification, by participation in the divine nature (see 2 Pt 1:4), is twofold: first, the supernatural transformation of the soul into God, through infused grace and charity, and, secondly, the supernatural union of this justified soul with God.

The Holy Spirit is thus not only present in the sanctified, through the operations of His abundant graces, that is, through the communication of created gifts, but He dwells substantially and personally in them as uncreated grace, that is, as Source and Dispenser of supernatural gifts, as well as the object of supernatural knowledge and love, direct possession and enjoyment.

Thus, as children and heirs of God (see Rom 8:17), we are elevated to an unspeakably intimate relationship with God, and are consequently equipped for a life truly divine.

This deification of man by God lays the foundation for a childlike and friendly relationship which implies the closest of contacts and the richest sharing of all goods.

The Holy Spirit comes to the just to remain with them, to be in them (see Jn 14:17), and to dwell with them (see Rom 8:9–27).

He comes not only at the time of a sinner's justification, that is, at the first infusion of sanctifying grace, but on the occasion of each richer communication of grace to the children of God.

Even those souls who already possess the Holy Spirit continue to repeat the cry that He may come to them and abide with them in steadily increasing measure, that He may impart His sanctifying grace in ever-greater abundance that they may be "transformed into the same image from glory to glory" (2 Cor 3:18).

Behold how the Holy Spirit, together with the Father and the Son, takes up His abode in the sanctified; inwardly, to be sure, as God in His own temple.

Says St. Augustine: "The entire Trinity—that is, the Father, the Son, and the Holy Spirit—come to us when we come to Them: They come helping, we obeying; They come enlightening, we to be enlightened; They come filling us, we to be filled in order that They may accord us not merely an external but an interior perception of Themselves, and that They may not merely bow to us in passing but that They may tarry with us eternally."[2]

The Holy Spirit descends from heaven to lay hold of the hearts of the faithful and to dower them with His gifts.

Through His dwelling and operations in the inmost depths of our soul, He establishes the spiritual life, which, being as well by its nature as by its origin and end, supernatural, heavenly, divine, and therefore mystic, is full of mystery. Our new and higher life which is ours from the Holy Spirit is here below "hid with Christ in God" from the eyes of the world; but when "Christ our Life" appears in His glory, then also the mysterious nobility of this present hidden life of grace will shine forth in full resplendent beauty and glory (see Col 3:3–4).

The supernatural life, though proper indeed to all the faithful who are in the state of grace, only blossoms into full flower in truly holy souls.

The term, "the spiritual life," however, is restricted solely to those who have reached an eminent degree of sanctity.

This life surpasses the ordinary life of the good and pious Christian, so called; it is really a perfectly rounded out interior existence. It stands out preeminently as the distinguished objective, and also as the most precious fruit, of the work of Christ and the operations of the Holy Spirit in the Church.

The Lord descended but once from the heights of heaven, but He still continues to send down the Holy Spirit that mankind may have the supernatural life and that in abundance (see Jn 10:10).

Still, not all Christians possessing the Holy Spirit lead a truly spiritual life; but only those who in all their undertakings allow themselves to be led by the Holy Spirit (see Rom 8:4), and accordingly walk in the Spirit (see Gal 5:16), and who, to this end, crucify their flesh with its passions and desires (see Gal 5:24), who love not the world (see 1 Jn 2:15), and are not of the world (see Jn 17:16), who look not at the things that are seen and are temporal (see 2 Cor 4:18), but who, with all their heart, center their affections on the eternal things that are above, where Christ sitteth at the right hand of the Father (see Col 3:1–2).

The spiritual life consists in the determined striving "to despise the passing things of earth" and "to love the heavenly," "in the relinquishing of the temporal and the tending ever toward the eternal."

Since, however, a ceaseless battle is ever raging between heavenly grace and depraved nature, between the spirit and the flesh, it is evident that only with supreme effort and exertion can the justified souls orientate themselves to a truly spiritual life. This is accomplished by generously embracing every opportunity and zealously cooperating with every grace in order to remain captains of our soul, even in legitimate matters, over "sensuality and mundane and earthly love."[3]

Hence an endless and all-out killing off of self is of prime moment to assure genuine progress and perseverance in the spiritual life.

Obstacles impeding our way must be pushed aside. We must vanquish our base inclinations and conquer nature's foibles to allow the Holy Spirit complete mastery over all the movements of our soul.

This accomplished, the spiritual life blossoms out before our eyes in majestic splendor. In its fruitage are included the possession and the operations of all the supernatural virtues, but their climax is reached only in the zealous practice of the three theological virtues.

These acts of faith, hope, and charity are so supernatural, so exalted and sublime, that through them we attain to a union with God at once most mystical, intimate, and rapturous.

As often as the Holy Spirit pervades a soul, He displays in that soul His grace-dispensing operations.

This request is now expressly beseeched: "And send forth from heaven a ray of Thy light."

Et emitte caelitus
Lucis tuae radium.

The light here longed for is characterized as both heavenly (*caelitus*) and divine (*lucis tuae radium*)—apart from the fact that the coming of the Holy Spirit has reference only to His producing supernatural effects.[4]

Light and life are one in God; the same is true in the world of grace, that is, the supernatural life is the supernatural light of man (see Jn 1:4). God Himself is the Source of life and in His light we shall see light (see Ps 35:10).

Thanks to these same graces, we are made partakers of the divine light and life.

The light under consideration here is, then, a supernatural gift which at the same time radiates from the luminous essence of the Holy Spirit and inwardly illumines, glorifies, and divinizes the soul.

Looked upon as the eternal, uncreated Light, the Holy Spirit is the Source of all supernatural life-giving light for man.

Cut off from its divine Source, the supernatural light of man would immediately be extinguished.

The Holy Spirit is imaged forth as a Fountainhead of light, as a shimmering Sea of light; as a Sun from Whose center rays not only emanate but constantly depend for their very existence.

"Uninterruptedly the divine Spirit's sun shines down mildly upon the Church like a continuous Pentecost, and, through the holy Sacraments and a thousand and one silent inspirations, He inundates the hearts of the faithful with the flood tide of His light and warmth."[5]

In Holy Scripture, no picture is employed so often as that of light in order to impress upon our mind more deeply what grace does and how grace operates.

The creative activity of the Holy Spirit is there shown as a radiating beam of grace converging upon our souls to transform them into supernatural images of His own holiness.

In the luminous brilliance that especially streams forth from light, we must note the glowing heat which is a property of fire.

Now it was this symbol of fire which the Holy Spirit chose for His own on the first Pentecost when He descended in a miraculous manner upon the apostles of the Lord.

Hence we find that it is not gleaming white but glowing red, which is the liturgical color of the Holy Spirit.

And so the Holy Spirit, as well inwardly in His nature as outwardly in His operations, is a fiery Light and a bright Fire.

The Holy Spirit is, then, a Fountain of light Whose rays penetrate, elevate, and beautify the innermost being of the soul, enlighten the mind with divine wisdom, and inflame the heart with heavenly warmth.

Thus penetrated with the light of the Holy Spirit, we partake in God's resplendent life of light and glory, are transformed into the divine image from glory to glory (see 2 Cor 3:18), are made light in the Lord and children of the Light (see Eph 5:8), and walk in the light of His countenance (see Ps 88:16).

The petition, "send forth Thy heavenly ray," is so general in tone that it embraces the complete supernatural workmanship of the Holy Spirit.

Yet He dispenses His gifts not only during the time of His actual indwelling but begins His reign long before. Indeed, it is so absolutely essential that He Himself furnishes the very first impulse to return to the path of rectitude. He does this by calling and drawing the erring soul through His prevenient grace. This invocation is therefore so pliable that it is applicable to all the faithful. It pertains to beginners in their return to, and entrance upon, the pathway of purgation; to the advanced who, under the clear light of heaven, go from virtue to virtue (see Ps 83:8), and climb the steep ascent of perfection; as likewise to those elect souls who have pitched their tent on the delightful, transcendent heights of mystical contemplation and union.

They all must incessantly entreat the Holy Spirit to illumine their eyes and hearts lest they succumb to the sleep of death and the enemy worst them (see Ps 12:4).[6]

Prayer alone, however, will not suffice to draw down upon us this precious, heavenly light; no, plus that we must eliminate all obstacles by keeping the eye of our soul ever clear and watchful.

True, it is always God Who begins the work in us, anticipating our efforts, but it is man's plain duty to follow through by loyal cooperation.

Where this is the case, the Holy Spirit pours forth His light, flooding our heart and soul in copious measure.

When obnoxious weeds have been torn out by the very roots, "the rays of the divine Sun shine upon the well-prepared field. Then we have a delightful summertime, a veritable blooming May, so familiar to the eye in that lovely month. In addition, the eternal God, through His Holy Spirit, produces bud, blossom, and the most luscious fruits, which neither tongue can describe nor heart contemplate—so abundant is the joy in our soul."[7] This is best substantiated in the lives of the saints. There the operations of the Holy Spirit met with the greatest response and the most wholehearted cooperation.

Examples without number could be cited to show that the hidden abundance of heavenly light in their hearts shone outwardly in wondrous ways, and was thus attested to by an unusual visible splendor.

To mention just a few: St. Francis Borgia, St. William of Oliva, Bl. Ambrose of Siena, St. Andrew of Avellini, St. Comgallus (d. 601, as abbot of Benchor in Ireland).

The true light, the "wondrous light" of the Holy Spirit, illumines all who are of good will.

Unfortunately, however, there are legions who put darkness for light and light for darkness (see Is 5:20), because they hate the light and love darkness (see Jn 3:19–20). Here in this life, they abide in the shadow of death (see Lk 1:79); and in the life beyond, they will be eternally excluded from the heavenly marriage feast and will be cast into exterior darkness (see Mt 25:30).

Blindness of heart, spiritual delusion, which turns voluntarily from the light, constitute a grave and well-nigh incurable malady.

"My God, enlighten my darkness" (Ps 17:29).

Veni, pater pauperum
(Come, O Father of the poor)

"Father of the poor"—this glorious title (even as all the other names of the Holy Spirit) is charged with sweetness and affability, with consolation and refreshment.

The name of *Father* here calls to mind all the paternal love, goodness, solicitude, forebearance, consideration, and benevolence with which the Holy Spirit continually dowers us poor children of men.

"As a father hath compassion on his children, so hath the Lord compassion on them that fear Him: for He knoweth our frame. He remembereth that we are dust.

"Man's days are as grass, as the flower of the field so shall he flourish. For the spirit shall pass in him, and he shall not be: and he shall know his place no more" (Ps 102:13–16).

Being weak and frail, humankind justly lays claim to the loving mercy of Him Who is styled, "Father of the poor."

The very reason of our weakness and insufficiency furnishes the motive for the Holy Spirit to bestow on us the love and mercy of a Father.[8]

Poverty-stricken is he who has few or very few earthly possessions; equally impoverished is he who is destitute of the higher spiritual goods. Spiritual, heavenly, and eternal goods are by far more excellent, more precious, and more conducive to happiness than anything the world might offer.

Now it is precisely in the possession of these exclusively spiritual goods, which are alone worth striving for, that all men are by nature exceedingly poor, and rendered still more destitute through personal sin.

"Remember not our former iniquities: let Thy mercies speedily prevent us, for we are become exceedingly poor" (Ps 78:8).

But only he who is keenly aware of his poverty in grace and virtue and yearns for the Kingdom of God and His justice, for "the one thing necessary" (see Lk 10:42), only such a one will experience the paternal benignity of the Holy Spirit, be blessed with spiritual riches, and dowered with imperishable treasures.

But one who fails to acknowledge that he is "miserable and poor and blind" but imagines that he is "rich and made wealthy and [has] need of nothing" (Apoc 3:17)—such a one will be sent empty away (see Lk 1:53).

To be filled with the spiritual gifts of the Holy Spirit, one must be "poor in spirit" (Mt 5:3), that is, he must possess the virtue of poverty. He must detach his heart from the vain, worthless goods of earth, and disengage it from all material, worldly, and sensual affections.

Whether one is impoverished or wealthy, interior renunciation and detachment are essential for the attainment of the kingdom of heaven promised to the poor.

The Spirit of the Lord anointed and sent the Savior to announce good tidings to the poor, to heal the contrite of heart, to give sight to the blind, to preach a release to the captive, and to console the sorrowful (see Is 61:1–5; and Lk 4:18–19).

"Blessed is he that understandeth concerning the needy and the poor" (Ps 40:2). This loving sympathy with those in distress and the alleviation of their misery and poverty are traceable to the Holy Spirit.

He continually pours forth into millions of souls genuine self-sacrificing love, which so resourcefully spends itself in trying to relieve all misery and woe. He is, therefore, the divine Fountainhead of all benignity and of all works of mercy.[9]

He it is Who by way of recompense imparts spiritual blessings "in full and overflowing measure" to all who generously bestow kindliness on others (see Lk 6:38).

The greater our spiritual poverty, the more undeserving we poor sinners are of the Holy Spirit's paternal kindness and benignity, the more ungrateful and culpable must be the one who resists (see Acts 7:51) and grieves Him (see Eph 4:30).[10]

Honor alone becomes so majestic, so princely, and so holy a Father.

Let us love so affable and benevolent a Father, and humble ourselves contritely for all our disloyalties in His service. The invocation, "Father of the poor," should therefore serve as an incentive for us to direct the following petitions to the Holy Spirit with childlike trust and confidence.

If the poor man cries out in this strain, the Lord hearkens to him and "[saves] him out of all his troubles" (Ps 33:7).

Remember how it is "easy in the eyes of God on a sudden to make the poor man rich" (Ecclus 11:23).

The Holy Spirit is not only infinitely merciful but also infinitely rich—rich, indeed, unto all who call upon Him (see Rom 10:12).[11]

Veni, dator munerum
(Come, Giver of gifts)

The "Father of the poor," Who is rich in mercy (see Eph 2:4), comes to remedy our poverty by imparting to us the supernatural gifts and graces of Christ.

From the manger to the Cross—from Bethlehem to Calvary—the Savior accumulated for all mankind a tremendous and inexhaustible treasury of merits and gathered together a superabundant wealth of graces for all.

Now all these spiritual goods are distributed through the agency of the Holy Spirit, Who divides to every one according as He will (see 1 Cor 12:11). The great apostle of the Gentiles, with unfeigned predilection and grateful wonderment, speaks not only of the riches of His grace (see Eph 1:7), and the riches of His glory (see

Rom 9:23; and Eph 3:16), but also of the overflowing riches of His grace (see Eph 2:7), and the unfathomable riches of Christ (see Eph 3:8).

It is the Holy Spirit Who is the Treasurer of Christ, and, through the conferring of these His (Christ's) riches, He works the sanctification of redeemed mankind, and effects the regeneration of the world. He bestows on us these very great and precious gifts of grace (see 2 Pt 1:4), which Christ purchased for us by His blood and through which we have been raised to the dignity, the liberty, and the glory of the children of God.

With jubilant enthusiasm, the young and beautiful Agnes, on the verge of martyrdom, portrays for us the incomparable splendor of the Holy Spirit's graces when she enumerates the dowry of her heavenly Bridegroom: "He has encircled my arm with a golden band and He has clasped my neck with a string of precious stones, put pearls beyond price in mine ears. With gay jewels He has adorned me. He has clothed me with a vesture of wrought gold. With many artistic adornments He has decked me and has shown me incomparable treasures to be mine (in heaven) if I persevere in His love."[12]

And so "every best gift and every perfect gift is from above" (Jas 1:17), that is, from the Holy Spirit "Who worketh all in all" (1 Cor 12:6). He attaches His graces to outward events as well as to those that interiorly agitate the soul, particularly crosses and sorrows, in order to turn the soul away from evil, from the commission of sin, and incline it to the practice of every Christian virtue. To Him is ascribed the beginning, the development, and the consummation of the work of salvation and perfection.

How often has He enlightened our mind with wholesome knowledge, moved our soul to pious feelings, and sweetly compelled our will to resolves and works that are pleasing to God!

Innumerable have been the moments of enlightenment and strength, of inspiration and encouragement with which His love has enriched all the days of our life. The efficacy of His grace continues ever onward in its effort to spread God's Kingdom externally in the world and to establish it interiorly in the hearts of men in order to bring it to ultimate perfection, (*ut in diebus nostris et merito et numero populus Dei serviens augeatur*[13]).

Therefore, be humble and grateful. Be mindful of the strict account you must render, of your heavy responsibility for "unto whomsoever much is given, of him much shall be required" (Lk 12:48).

And so "Bless the Lord, O my soul, and never forget all He hath done for thee.

"Who forgiveth all thy iniquities; Who healeth all thy diseases.

"Who redeemeth thy life from destruction; Who crowneth thee with mercy and compassion.

"Who satisfieth thy desire with good things" (Ps 102:2–5).

As an outpouring of fervent desire, our cry is persevering, ardent, and importunate. Therefore, summing up all previous petitions in one single prayer, we give utterance at the end of the verse by saying:

Veni, lumen cordium.
(Come, Light of hearts.)

How fertile in thought, how arresting are these words! The Holy Spirit, like a spiritual Sun, sends down His heavenly rays.

In very truth, He is "the Light of hearts," both in His operations and in His essence, for, together with His illuminating rays, He gives Himself as the perennial Wellspring of Immortal Light.

He is in the fullest sense, in the most sublime manner, "the Light of hearts" by letting His own personal life stream in upon them, that is, by infusing into their minds the light of supernatural knowledge and breathing into them a supernatural love.

O sublime, consoling, sweet mystery! "The light is sweet, and it is delightful for the eyes to see the sun" (Eccles 11:7). Hence the blind Tobias complains: "What manner of joy shall be to me, who sit in darkness and see not the light of heaven?" (Tb 5:12). Though great indeed be the excellencies, and splendid the qualities, of even earthly light which plays to the eye, one day to be broken and closed by death, still by comparison with the supernatural, heavenly Light of grace, Whose splendor will know no dimming, it is immeasurably inferior. This "marvelous light" of God (1 Pt 2:9) constitutes the life and delight of immortal hearts, whereas that other light of the senses is but a passing joy for mortal man.

In comparison with other physical phenomena, visible light is preeminently the most perfect symbol to portray the invisible, other-worldly Sun of graces.

But when all is said, we still have a very vague and imperfect image of those incomparable spiritual goods of grace that God Himself acquired for us with His own blood (see Acts 20:28).

A ray of pure white light breaks up into the most divergent colors and surpasses all other created objects by the sheer splendor of its qualities—purity, clarity, brightness, swiftness, elegance, and beauty—as well as by its powerful effects: it gives light and warmth; it vivifies, delights, and beautifies.

Hence the language of Scripture and of the Church makes use of it as the most perfect symbol of divine grace. Although by its very nature grace is but one, "she can do all things: and ... reneweth all things" (Ws 7:27).

Grace branches out and diffuses itself into manifold virtues, gifts, beatitudes, and fruits, and produces an inexhaustible wealth of blessings in our souls.

Thus "all good things came to me together with her, and innumerable riches through her hands" (Ws 7:11). "For she is an infinite treasure to men: which they that use, become the friends of God" (Ws 7:14).

When the Holy Spirit, Who, at the Creation of the world, "commanded the light to shine out of darkness, hath shined in our hearts" (2 Cor 4:6), then too desolation and darkness disappear, to give way to a paradise abounding in life, beauty, and bliss.

"When the sun rises brightly in a cloudless summer sky, what rich fruits does it not bring forth from the earth by its clear bright light and by its powers!

"See how the meadows become green, how the foliage and grass sprout forth, how the beautiful flowers laugh in their colorful array!

"How the woods and heath and meadow resound with the sweet notes of the nightingale and of the birds!"[14] This is a picture of the bountiful springtime of virtue awakened and called forth in the depths of our heart by the Holy Spirit.

The "Enlightenment of the Holy Spirit instructs the hearts of the faithful" in the most perfect manner, for through it not only is truth disclosed to the intellect but love is likewise enkindled in the will toward the recognized truth thus acquired.

His blissful, heavenly instruction illumines and warms the heart.

Here we have a case in point of that invisible, spiritual anointing which sincere believers have "from the Holy One" and which teaches them concerning all things (see 1 Jn 2:20–27).

A clean heart receives the light of understanding directly from above.

The words spoken interiorly by the Holy Spirit enlighten the understanding, inflame the heart, excite it to compunction, and afford manifold consolations.[15] When the Holy Spirit illumines, strengthens, and animates us interiorly with the light of His grace, then our oppressed and constricted hearts awaken and expand with a new spontaneity in jubilant enthusiasm.

We can then run the way of the commandments with the greatest ease as we courageously surmount all obstacles impeding the pathway of virtue (see Ps 118:32).

When the Lord fills thy soul with brightness, then shall thy light rise up in darkness and thy darkness shall be as the noonday (see Is 58:10–11).

When the Holy Spirit dwells in thee, thy heart shall wonder and be enlarged with a blissful happiness (see Is 60:5).

"When the bright morning star arises in my inmost soul, then every grief vanishes, all darkness disappears, giving way to unruffled serenity. Then, indeed, O Lord, my heart frolics, my whole being rejoices, my soul exults. I am so buoyant that everything in me and about me unites in one grand hymn to chant Thy praises.

"What was difficult, laborious, and impossible becomes easy and sweet. Fasting, watching, praying, suffering, shunning evil, and all austerity are completely destroyed, that is, seem as nothing, in Thy holy presence.

"The soul is flooded with enlightenment and truth as to be oblivious of all toil.

"The heart experiences perceptible sweetness in meditation; the tongue is steeped in eloquence, the body addresses itself with facility to every task.

"I seem to have transcended all time and space and to stand in the antechamber of eternal blessedness.

"What then does the soul seek exteriorly, since it carries concealed within its own bosom the kingdom of heaven?

"Truly the kingdom of heaven is joy and peace in the Holy Spirit."[16]

The Son proceeds from the Father as "Light from Light."

From the light of the Father and the Son, the Holy Spirit proceeds as a Fire of Love, as a Divine Person.

O that our cold hearts would be inflamed at this glowing Furnace of all true, surpassing, supernatural love!

May the heavenly fire that the Savior brought on earth be enkindled in us ever more and more! (see Lk 12:49). In the saints, this fire of love was aflame and burned with such ardor and intensity that even the physical heart itself was often affected, in a most unusual manner. Not only their souls but even their bodies rejoiced in the living God (see Ps 83:3). We recall, for instance, the case of a St. Stanislaus Kostka, a St. Mary Magdalene of Pazzi, and especially a St. Philip Neri.

We all know that the absence of light connotes darkness, which signifies a state of spiritual misery, of religious ignorance and unhappiness, even as light symbolizes happiness, blessing, salvation, and everything that is amiable and beautiful. Hence one may easily realize how staggering and enormous are the evils and dangers threatening a soul plunged in the night of darkness, because bereft of the light of grace (see Rom 1:21).

To all are addressed the words of St. Paul, warning the Christians "walk not as also the Gentiles walk in the vanity of their mind: having their understanding darkened: being alienated from the life of God through the ignorance that is in them, because of the blindness of their hearts" (Eph 4:17–18).

Let us be on our guard so as not to extinguish the heavenly light of the Holy Spirit within us (see 1 Thes 5:19), lest dark night enshroud our hearts and we be swallowed up in the eternal night of hell. Let us not cease to meditate upon the law of the Lord (see Ps 1:2) and to pray for enlightenment and for deliverance from all blindness of heart.[17]

"The Lord is my light and my salvation, whom shall I fear?" (Ps 26:1).

Second Stanza (Literal Translation)

Thou best Consoler,
Sweet Guest of the soul,
Sweet Coolness
In labor, Rest;
In heat, Refreshment;
In tears, Solace.

Until that day when pain and mourning shall be no more, until we arrive at the land of eternal joy and gladness (see Is 35:10), until the day of eternity dawns and the morning star arises in our hearts, we are wanderers by faith in a dark place (see 2 Pt 1:19).

On this pilgrim's journey through a strange land to our heavenly home, we stand sorely in need of a true comforter, for "the life of man upon earth is a warfare, and his days are like the days of a hireling.

"As a servant longeth for the shade, as the hireling looketh for the end of his work" (Jb 7:1–2).

In this frame of mind, we now call out to the Holy Spirit:

Consolator optime
(Come, Consoler the Best)

All the consolations of the Holy Spirit have this in common: that through their beneficent, invigorating, and refreshing influence on the soul, they assuage sorrow, pain, and sadness, making them less burdensome and not infrequently render them lighter and more agreeable.

The Holy Spirit is the God of all comfort Who comforts us in all our afflictions (see 2 Cor 1:3–4). Through His being sent, this promise of God found its fulfillment: "I Myself will comfort you" (Is 51:12), "and your heart shall rejoice" (Jn 16:22).

By making us partakers of His endless joys, the Holy Spirit fulfills beautifully, in our regard, the role of "Comforter the Best."

This is so because His might parallels His love and mercy and He is, consequently, in a position to impart His precious consolation in most wonderful fashion and in unstinted measure.

The comfort which He affords surpasses every earthly solace.

His is a spiritual, supernatural comfort and is handed on to the Christian to further the salvation and sanctification of his soul.

To be sure, one can and should solace one's neighbor, since it is written: "Be not wanting in comforting them that weep, and walk with them that mourn" (Ecclus 7:38), and the apostle likewise admonishes: "Comfort the feeble minded" (1 Thes 5:14). But whereas we can only cheer up, encourage, and sustain our neighbor by external exhortation, the Holy Spirit can awaken in the depths of the human heart a joyful, confident, and determined disposition of soul.

This He effects by imparting light and understanding to the mind, and by flooding the will with strength, trust, and peace.

For this reason, the Holy Spirit is the Source of all true comfort.

He consoles in an interior, abiding, and salutary fashion, whereas the world's comforts are merely earthly, superficial, and fleeting.[18]

Hence to those, who neither sense the need of the consolations of the Holy Spirit nor yet cherish a desire for them, but who seek their happiness solely in riches and the pleasures they afford—to these the Savior addresses these words: "Woe to you rich: for you have your consolation" (Lk 6:24).

The world is powerless to bestow a consolation that is truly joy-imparting.

On the other hand, so wholesome, so refreshing, so strengthening, so blessed is the comfort of the Holy Spirit that it lightens life's burdens marvelously, soothes all pain, and sweetens all bitterness.

"When the Holy Spirit, abiding within us, fills the soul with His delightful splendor and floods it with His divine light, when He Who is called and is in very truth the true Comforter is allowed to exercise the sweet potency of His sway—O what surpassing joy!

"To experience even so much as one little drop of this consolation surpasses, in range of sweetness and taste, all that creatures could offer.

"The one partaking of but a single drop of this perceptible grace would be so flooded with purest joy that the winning of heaven would become as easy for him as the avoidance of hell will be difficult for the other who enjoys to the full the world with its cunning deceits and evil sanctions."[19]

Personal experience alone can teach one what a precious gift from heaven "the hidden manna" (Apoc 2:17) of these spiritual consolations truly is. "O taste, and see that the Lord is sweet" (Ps 33:9). In like manner, all true solace that comes to us from others has its ultimate source in the Holy Spirit.

The Spirit of the Lord anointed the Redeemer in His human nature to preach glad tidings to the meek, to heal the contrite of heart, to comfort them that mourn (see Is 61:1–2), to give rest to all that labor and are burdened (see Mt 11:28), that is, to impart to them light and strength, to bring them peace of heart and rest of soul.

Through a rich bestowal of grace, the Holy Spirit made the Blessed Virgin Mary "the Mother of Mercy" and "the Comforter of the afflicted" for us poor children of Eve.

The Holy Spirit spoke through the prophets and inspired the holy men of God (see 2 Pt 1:21) that we might have for our comfort the holy books (see 1 Mc 12:9) and that through the comfort of the Scripture we might have hope (see Rom 15:4).

Finally, the Holy Spirit also fills all apostolic men with heavenly wisdom and love and eloquence that they may be qualified to comfort others through instructive and inspirational encouragement.

In fulfilling this role, they are merely the instruments of the "Consoler the Best" Who, through their words, addresses Himself to the inmost heart.

These spiritual consolations should be highly esteemed, for they are priceless; moreover, they are absolutely necessary for a devout life, especially for the striving after higher perfection.

Short though life may be, it often seems protracted because of a host of miseries and afflictions, of heavy crosses and bitter sorrows that must be endured. As a result, we often find ourselves yielding to sadness and melancholy, bordering even on the verge of despair and despondency.

We stand, then, in dire need of a divine Consoler and of heavenly comforts as long as we are wayfarers and exiled from the Lord, we who in this tent sigh for deliverance from this mortality (see 2 Cor 5:1–6), that what is mortal may be swallowed up by life.

Without interior comfort, without the light and strength of the Holy Spirit, we are powerless to bear up patiently, courageously, and joyfully in the face of the manifold sorrows, afflictions, and tribulations of this life, which the attainment of the kingdom of heaven imposes on us (see Acts 14:21).

The true servant of God is called upon to renounce, not only the forbidden, but, in many instances, even the legitimate pleasures and joys of the world. Only when fortified through an abundance of graces and refreshed by spiritual joys will the human heart be capable of achieving this degree of sacrifice and renunciation for any great length of time.

"The spiritual unction" of the Holy Spirit alone can supply the strength essential to the disciple yearning for perfection in order to persevere in the occasionally difficult, rough, burdensome, and bristling highway of prayer, mortification, and penance without weakening or even succumbing before the lofty peak is reached.

The Church in her liturgy points out to us the manner of invoking, and the admonition often to invoke, the consolations of the Holy Spirit.

But these petitions will only then be efficacious if we are generous in overcoming ourselves in order to remove from our hearts all hindrances to these consolations. Hence we must not only be heartily sorry for all our sins and do penance for them, but we must be ever alert in combatting all inordinate attachments to the goods and pleasures of earth, all distractions, lukewarmness, and sloth in the service God.

Only a humble and pure heart is susceptible to the inner comforts and favors of the Holy Spirit. These are especially conferred in rich profusion on the dutiful performance of the daily exercises of devotion and piety as, for example, at the time of meditation, of spiritual reading, on the occasion of one's visits to the Blessed Sacrament, attendance at Holy Mass, and the reception of the Sacraments.

In proportion as the soul's generosity is greater in spurning all human and earthly consolation, and the more resolute in suffering, working, and campaigning for God and His Kingdom, so much the richer will be the visitations of the Holy Spirit, and the sweet refreshments vouchsafed through His grace.

Thus a truly Christian life—above all in its more advanced stages—despite troubles and afflictions is in reality full of heavenly joy and bliss.

In this sense, the apostle exclaims: "I am filled with comfort: I exceedingly abound with joy in all our tribulation" (2 Cor 7:4).

"For as the sufferings of Christ abound in us, so also by Christ doth our comfort abound" (2 Cor 1:5).

The Holy Spirit bestows upon the faithful, in the celebration and participation of the liturgical year, an abiding fullness of consolation. This should be for all a year of salvation and holiness, ever and anon repeating itself.

The complete history of our salvation, the epitome of the redemptive plan from its gracious beginning, to its blessed development, and on to its eternal consummation, is reenacted before our eyes in the divine service in the course of the liturgical year. The one objective of all this is that man may more and more immerse his mind and heart in the joyful, the sorrowful, and the glorious mysteries comprising the lives of Jesus and Mary.

Manger! Cross! Altar!

Are not these three monuments of the merciful and redeeming love of God an exhaustless fountain of light and life, of salvation and blessing?

He who, in this spirit, celebrates the feasts of the Church and observes her days of penance with intelligent and interior participation must of necessity wax strong in the virtues of faith, hope, and charity—these fountainheads of spiritual joy. Such souls emancipate themselves ever more from earthly desires, seek ever more the things that are eternal, and take pleasure and delight only in divine and spiritual goods. This is that "everlasting consolation" spoken of by the apostle (2 Thes 2:15).

The Church in her liturgy shows a preference for the use of the word *Paraclete* (Comforter).[20]

Now our most perfect comforter, our divine consoler, full of might and tenderness, is none other than the Holy Spirit, comforting us in every affliction, in every grief and sadness of this mortal life.

He carries out this program not only by dispensing light and strength from on high, but even more effectively by a personal visit and by abiding in our soul as "a charming, intimate, and sweet Guest."

Dulcis hospes animae
(Come, our bosom's dearest Guest)

A mystery of divine love, at once heartening and profound, is expressed in this frequently used figure of speech, namely, that the Holy Spirit, in an indescribably intimate and gracious manner, is a divine Visitor, a fatherly Friend, and at the same time the majestic Lord of the human soul.

Who can sufficiently marvel at this lovely mystery? "What is a man, that Thou shouldst magnify him or why dost Thou set Thy heart upon him?" (Jb 7:17). Quite expressive is that word *hospes* (Guest, intimate) since it indicates, in touching fashion, the special relation established between the Holy Spirit and the favored soul.

Let us explain. The Holy Spirit dwells on high (see Ps 112:5). Heaven is His throne (see Is 66:1). Hence the human soul is for Him a strange abode. He really enters there as a "Guest." To make a worthy dwelling place for this exalted Guest, the soul, through grace, must be elevated to a supernatural likeness to God, that is, it must be not only purified, but likewise sanctified and adorned.

In a soul thus exalted through participation in the divine nature (see 2 Pt 1:4), the Holy Spirit now dwells not merely as a Guest but as a condescending intimate Bosom-Friend.

In fine, grace makes holy souls the friends of God (see Ws 7:27; 7:14; and Jn 15:14–15), for it establishes such a supernatural likeness between them that a friendly, that is, a most intimate, confidential relationship is rendered possible. For this reason, the psalmist bursts forth in admiration with the words: "But to me Thy friends, O God, are made exceedingly honorable" (Ps 138:17).

The Holy Spirit wills not only to confer on us a mark of distinction by His presence, but also to enrich us and give us joy through the priceless treasure of heavenly goods that He bestows on us with divine munificence.

No friendship of earth can compare with this divine friendship, for between the Holy Spirit and the favored children of God there exists a friendship most tender and delightful.

He comes, let us recall, not as a mere Visitor, but as a permanent Guest. He tarries with us, namely, not for a short span of time but in order to dwell with us forever. (*Ut maneat nobiscum in aeternum*—Jn 14:16). His charming presence abides in the soul as long as we preserve sanctifying grace. This grace should be highly esteemed for the further reason that it not only introduces into our soul so sublime a Guest, but likewise unites us most intimately with Him.

Nothing, save only mortal sin, can drive this divine Guest from the soul, and therefore the warning of the apostle is applicable to all the justified: "Grieve not the Holy Spirit of God" (Eph 4:30). The joyous exuberance, the affability, and bliss incident to this friendly relationship, are here expressly emphasized since the Holy Spirit is praised as "the sweet Guest of the soul."

"O how good and sweet is Thy Spirit, O Lord, in us" (see Ws 12:1)—thus the Church sings in the Mass for the Friday after Pentecost.

The Holy Spirit is infinite Love, Goodness, Mildness, and Sweetness. Hence, dwelling with Him in the same abode renders association with Him devoid of everything that connotes bitterness or unpleasantness; on the contrary, it produces only holy joy and happiness (see Ws 8:16).

"How great is the multitude of Thy sweetness, O Lord, which Thou hast hidden for them that fear Thee!" (Ps 30:20).

One can have an inkling of this mystical, otherworldly sweetness only after having felt and tasted it through personal experience.

The Holy Spirit gives Himself as the Object of immediate possession and enjoyment. Here below, as long as we walk by faith, we can by supernatural vision and love experience and come to know of His presence, but only in our eternal home above will the soul be inebriated and satiated by the stream and torrent of heavenly joy (see Ps 16:15; and 35:9).

Through His gracious condescension, the Holy Spirit elevates us to a divine friendship, to a most intimate fellowship of life and love with the Father and the Son (see 1 Jn 1:3), and thus our heart is the dwelling place of the Holy Spirit and consequently of the Blessed Trinity.

Thanks to the divine indwelling, we are sanctified, that is, our soul, and even our body, becomes a consecrated dwelling place, a sanctuary, and a temple of the Holy Spirit.

"Do you not know that you are the temple of God and that the Spirit of God dwelleth in you? But if any man violate the temple of God, him shall God destroy. For the temple of God is holy, which you are" (1 Cor 3:16–17).

"Know you not that your members are the temple of the Holy Ghost, Who is in you, Whom you have from God: and you are not your own?" (1 Cor 6:19).

In this sense not only the soul but also the body shares an inviolable consecration and dignity as the temple of the Holy Spirit. Indeed, because of the indwelling of the Holy Spirit—*propter inhabitantem Spiritum in nobis*—(Rom 8:11), our own mortal body will be raised up to a glorious life and will be changed into a spiritual body (see 1 Cor 15:44).

"The Lord is in His holy temple" (Ps 10:5), that is to say, the Holy Spirit Who has laid claim to us as His own possession, desires ever to be accorded all the adoration, reverence, and homage that is His due as the Spirit of glory (see 1 Pt 4:14).

The fact of the indwelling (engracement of the soul) cannot be ascertained here below—apart from a special revelation—with the infallible certainty of faith, a fact which should fill us with a wholesome fear. Certain signs are at hand, however, that make it more or less probable, even morally certain, that we possess the Holy Spirit and His seven gifts.[21]

These signs are simply the working of the Holy Spirit which He Himself effects in our heart and actions. They afford us comforting peace and assurance.

Such signs are, for example, the testimony of a good conscience, of having fulfilled all the conditions necessary for the forgiveness of our sins, peace of soul and composure of spirit, contempt of the world and of all mundane vanities, love for the Word of God as well as for heavenly things, energetic striving for growth in grace and for constant advance in virtue—in a word, self-sacrifice in all sufferings and labors in the interests of Christ and His Church, all works of fraternal charity, of zeal for souls, and deeds of piety.

The Holy Spirit is likewise our Comfort insofar as, in virtue of His personal presence, He is the Pledge of our heavenly inheritance (see Eph 1:14).

Again from the fact that He gives Himself to be enjoyed through holy love, He tenders us not only a foretaste of heavenly joy but accords us at the same time a certain assurance of the full happiness and glory of heaven through the immediate vision of the triune God.

Now only a divine pledge can guarantee a divine inheritance—an inheritance that is reserved for us in heaven and is therefore incorruptible, undefiled, and unfading (see 1 Pt 1:4). The frequent pondering of this sublime article of faith would help mightily toward the promotion of recollection and the cultivation of the interior life.

But alas how anemic is our spirit of faith!

It is the delight of the Holy Spirit to be with the children of men (see Prv 8:31). Should it not likewise be our delight to hold sweet communion with Him?

"If we were always conscious of the distinguished Guest Whom we harbor within us, it would be impossible to abandon ourselves so blindly to earthly things, for we would come to realize only too well their cheapness in comparison to the things that we bear within ourselves."[22]

Would that we were experts in the art of conversing in holy simplicity with this divine Guest—in greeting, adoring, praising, and entreating Him now as our Creator and Lord, now as our Father and Benefactor, now as our Friend and Consoler, now as our Master, and now as our Counselor.

But how often our heart resembles a marketplace where all is topsy-turvy. Why should we not convert it into a chapel where quiet and peace would reign and where the frivolous turmoil of the world would be excluded?

This interior way of life does not shackle efficiency, but purifies, governs, and sanctifies exterior activity.

The Holy Spirit does not limit His calls to the time of regeneration, but He often visits the children of God, above all, when He grants them the grace of devotion.

Let us then resolve to cling to Him. "Stay with us, because it is towards evening and the day is now far spent" (Lk 24:29)—thus spoke the two disciples to the Lord on the way to Emmaus.

He complied and sat down to table with them not so much in the role of Guest, but rather in the character of Father and Host.

May we also pray to the Holy Spirit to tarry ever with us as our sweet Friend and Consoler, especially in dark and sad moments, but above all when the day of our life approaches its setting and the end of our pilgrimage draws near.

Intimacy with the Holy Spirit especially yields high dividends because from it we can draw strength and courage for all our temptations, and refreshment for all the sufferings and battles of life.

This thought is again repeated and developed in the verse:

Dulce refrigerium.
(Come, sweet Refreshment.)

For the sake of coherence, it is best to understand these words as the completion of the preceding figure of speech.

The Holy Spirit is our "sweet Guest" but in such a way that He Himself prepares the "sweet repast"[23] for the soul into which He enters. "In Thy sweetness, O God, Thou hast provided for the poor" (Ps 67:11).

This spiritual repast is the interior communing with the divine Guest from which the soul feeds, on which the soul is refreshed, and within which the soul experiences indescribable happiness.

Through His intimate indwelling and operations, the Holy Spirit is for the soul the Source of all heavenly light and divine power, of all her true possessions through which she is refreshed, invigorated, and gladdened until the invitation is issued summoning her to the marriage supper of the Lamb (see Apoc 19:9).

"The world is full of treachery, deceit, and inconstancy. Even friendship's death knell sounds when friendship's usefulness is gone. To put it in a few words: no heart ever found in a creature unalloyed love, nor perfect happiness, nor abiding peace of soul.

"The tiniest elusive joy that man occasionally captures soon sours; for it is acquired with effort, is enjoyed with anxious fear, and, alas, is lost amid poignant bitterness."[24]

Earth after all is but a spot in space, and life upon it a period of labor, of combat, and of suffering.

From these labors, the Holy Spirit does not free us here below, but He comforts us in them to the degree that we accept them willingly from the hand of God, even rejoice in them (see Col 1:24) and come to glory in them (see 2 Cor 12:5–9).

In labore requies[25] *(Rest in labor)*

Work and rest are contradictory, for he who rests ceases to work and enjoys repose from labor. But the Holy Spirit even here below accords true rest to the soul at work and during work.[26]

"Why seekest thou rest, since thou art born to labor?"[27]

By nature man is prone to shrink from burdensome and fatiguing labor and inclined to yearn for the peaceful, comforting enjoyment of the goods and joys of this life. Yet earnest and unremitting labor is the lifelong task of the children of Adam.

Without dutiful application to this life's task on earth, there will be no eternal rest in heaven. "Cursed is the earth in thy work: with labor and toil shalt thou eat thereof all the days of thy life.... In the sweat of thy face shalt thou eat bread" (Gn 3:17, 19).

This just sentence pronounced upon our forefather pertains likewise to his sinful descendants. Since then, man is born to labor as the bird to fly (see Jb 5:7), work since that moment assumes for man, banished from the garden of paradise, the form of penance.

By work undertaken in time, man must merit for himself rest in eternity. Of the reprobate it is written: "And the smoke of their torments, shall ascend up for ever and ever: neither have they rest day nor night" (Apoc 14:11). And so let us bestir ourselves by an active life of virtue to enter into the heavenly Sabbath-rest—into the full, sublime, glorious rest of God (see Ps 94:11; and Heb 3:7–4:11).

"Nature loveth leisure and bodily ease; but grace cannot be idle and willingly embraceth labor."[28] Only when the night of death breaks in upon us, wherein no man can merit more, will the Spirit bid us rest from our labors (see Apoc 14:13); but, while life is granted us in which we can work (see Jn 9:4), He spurs us on to untiring activity and industry.

Since here below "the corruptible body is a load upon the soul, and the earthy habitation presseth down the mind" (Ws 9:15), the labors that confront us are, as a rule, wearisome and fatiguing.

The Holy Spirit is, however, at hand to ease these burdens through His manifold graces (see 1 Pt 4:10) in virtue of which He is with us and labors with us (see Ws 9:10). Of course, a well-balanced, systematic program of work is richly remunerative in pure enjoyment—the more so if it comes as a result of long, habitual practice—and functions along with a minimum degree of friction, but even this will not suffice to overcome all obstacles. Natural repugnance to all that requires exertion and labor will only be permanently vanquished through the supernatural assistance of the Holy Spirit. He makes the yoke of labor so light and restful that it will not gall, and so eases the burden of work that it will not be oppressive (see Mt 11:30).

Through grace, man is made a "new creature" (2 Cor 5:17). Through a virtuous life, he acquires the ability, the proficiency, the inclination, and through the gifts of the Holy Spirit, a certain facility, to work cheerfully in the vineyard of the Lord (see Mt 20:1). With such perfection does he carry on that the virtuous acts, produced through the energetic help of the gifts of the Holy Spirit, appear as "beatitudes" and as sweet "fruits."

In addition, we are the recipients of a wealth of actual graces that lend to the enfeebled will such a steadfast buoyance, that we do not grow weary and lose heart (see Heb 12:3), but courageously bear the burden of the heat and the day (see Mt 20:12), until the festive evening descends on us to lead us into eternal rest.

Thus we find peace of soul in the midst of our toils (see Mt 11:29), for the Holy Spirit, through the light and strength of His grace, not only helps us overcome the ennui attendant upon our more serious vocational work, but He likewise infuses joy and happiness into those trials at which nature only too soon and too often is wont to complain.

The more the dominance of nature is suppressed, through the power of grace, and the greater the advance on the pathway of virtue and perfection, the more ardent grows our love and enthusiasm for good works and sacrifices of all kinds.

Hence, just those Christians, who in a noble and generous spirit bear up under the welter of hardships and vexations of their high calling, enjoy on this earth a refreshing peace of soul that is a participation in that endlessly blessed, and, at the same time, ceaselessly active, rest of God. We grant, though, that the consolations of the Holy Spirit are not always perceptible. Very often, even the holiest of souls experience keenly and painfully the manifold shortcomings, the unavoidable demands and burdens of this workaday world. But precisely in these dark moments, the Holy Spirit sustains their courage and their determination of will with the blessed prospect and conviction that, though labor oppresses them for a short period, a blessed rest, on the contrary, will be their portion through endless ages.

Above all other virtues, it is the burning love of God and of neighbor which not only impels us to indefatigable activity (see 2 Cor 5:14), but even renders the burdens of labor light and pleasant.

The whole life of Jesus upon earth was one of poverty and hardship.

Fatigued from His daily work, the God-Man ate His bread in the sweat of His brow and thus, thanks to His divine example, work has been ennobled and sanctified. Accordingly, let every one work earnestly and perseveringly in his own avocation as a good soldier of Christ (see 2 Tm 2:3), for our labor in the Lord is not in vain (see 1 Cor 15:58), since each will receive his own reward according to his labor (see 1 Cor 3:8).

God gives "to the just the wages of their labors" (Ws 10:17), "for the fruit of good labors is glorious" (Ws 3:15) even in time, but more so in eternity.

Those only and strictly those who labor untiringly in the service of God will experience rest even here below; this is obviously not an indolent, indulgent rest, but a rest bringing peace in its wake to the soul. On the completion of their earthly span of labor, the Spirit of God will pension them with eternal rest in recompense for their labors (see Apoc 14:13). "Who will give me wings like a dove, and I will fly and be at rest?" (Ps 54:7). Patience, then, poor afflicted soul! "Expect the Lord" patiently (Ps 26:14), for the days of your earthly sojourn will soon be over.

Then you will cry out, in exultation: "Turn, O my soul, into thy rest: for the Lord hath been bountiful to thee" (Ps 114:7). In the realms above the People of God "shall sit in the beauty of peace, and in the tabernacles of confidence, and in wealthy rest" (Is 32:18).[29]

The labor of the combat (*labor certaminis*[30]) against the passions is especially wearisome, even as evil concupiscence itself is for man a great torment and misery.

"What is more annoying in this life than to be consumed with earthly desires?" asks St. Isidore. Therefore in this distress we cry out to the Holy Spirit, for He is in truth:

In aestu temperies
(Coolness in the midst of heat)

The expression *aestus* (stifling, oppressive sultry heat) is here to be taken in a figurative sense.

Insofar as it conjures up the picture of a seething caldron bubbling over, it masterfully portrays the restlessness of human appetites and passions.

Here are especially meant those emotions which are awakened through enticing objects falling under our senses and which, as a consequence, very easily and often transgress the bounds of morality and for the quelling of which we stand in need of the Holy Spirit and His blessed assistance.[31]

Sensual inclinations and tendencies very often arouse undue excitement and confusion in weak human beings; concupiscence, we know, remains a lifelong struggle even after our spiritual rebirth in Baptism.

It is beyond man's unaided power to wage so difficult, dangerous, and protracted a struggle to a victorious conclusion; to achieve this end, he stands sorely in need of divine assistance.

"I cannot resist the passions of sensuality unless Thy most holy grace, infused into my heart, assist me.

"There is need of Thy grace, O Lord, and of a great measure thereof, that nature may be overcome which is ever prone to evil from its youth."[32]

Man's principal task on earth is precisely this: that, as far as possible, he shall restore to his soul, through the practice of asceticism—or vigorous spiritual combat—the peaceful, harmonious, and blessed state which was the special gift of God to our first parents, and which, in the eternal designs, they were to transmit to their descendants.

But in consequence of the Fall, this precious, heavenly gift was lost to all men, excepting the Blessed Virgin. Through faithful and zealous cooperation, however, with the rich and powerful grace of God, we can regain, in some measure, the former blissful state our first parents enjoyed in paradise, but never fully attain it.

In a variety of ways, the Holy Spirit assists our manifold weakness (see Rom 8:26). He dowers us with the supernatural virtue of temperance, which qualifies and disposes us to reduce our sensual inclinations to their proper status and to keep them well in hand.

In addition, we are equipped with the gift of fear, which helps us in mastering concupiscence more easily and efficiently. To practice this virtue of temperance is binding on all.

But one who is intent on gaining the complete victory of the spirit over the flesh must not rest on his laurels; he must deny himself even in legitimate matters. This struggle against base and earthly inclinations will culminate in speedier victory and interior peace the more generously the Holy Spirit strengthens and justifies the combatant through His heavenly inspirations and consolations and through the grace of devotion and compunction of heart.

"For spiritual comforts exceed all the delights of the world and the pleasures of the flesh.

"Grant that I may die to all things that are in the world; Thou art the true peace of the heart; Thou are its only rest; out of Thee all things are full of trouble and difficulty."[33]

In like manner as the Holy Spirit tempers the fires of concupiscence and the ardor of the passions, so does He at times soothe the burning pain and torments occasioned by fire. In this respect, the word *aestus* can be taken literally.

Numerous instances in the Martyrology furnish ample evidence in this regard.

"Fear not, ... thou art Mine. When thou shalt walk in the fire, thou shall not be burnt, and the flames shall not burn in thee" (Is 43:1–2).

Thou hast delivered me "from the oppression of the flame which surrounded me, and in the midst of the fire I was not burnt" (Ecclus 51:6), so prays Jesus the son of Sirach.

With buoyant enthusiasm, St. Lawrence from his fiery bed, the gridiron, cried out to the tyrant: "Learn, O miserable man, what is the power of God: for your fire is like a cooling draught to me, but in your case it will become an everlasting furnace."

While St. Tiburtius walked barefoot over glowing coals, he said to the judge: "Your coals seem like flowers to me."[34]

A variety of symbols suggest this cooling and refreshing activity (*temperies*) of the Holy Spirit.

On the Mount of Transfiguration, for instance, the Holy Spirit appeared visibly under the form of a bright cloud, which simultaneously emitted light and cast a shadow. In the same way, as that cloud overshadowed the three disciples, is the Holy Spirit now for us a bright cooling Cloud shielding us from the scorching heat (see Is 25:4), for He refreshes and regales us when the fierce heat of passion and pain would consume us.

Other symbols of the Holy Spirit, respectively of His activity, are the sound of the wind (on the first Pentecost), and water (for example, in Baptism). Their action is similar to that of the cloud casting a cooling shadow over the burning heat.

The stanza closes, as it began, with the verse:

In fletu solatium.
(Comfort in our woe.)

All human comfort can boast of but one quality: it is empty and fleeting.

Blessed only is the solace communicated to the human heart by the Holy Spirit.

We repeat this truth once more with emphasis.

"Wherefore, O my soul, thou canst not have full comfort nor perfect delight except in God, the Comforter of the poor and the Helper of the humble."[35]

Not they that laugh but they that mourn and weep will be comforted by God (see Mt 5:5; and Lk 6:25).

Weeping betokens deep sorrow or at least a commingling of emotions that include a profound disturbance of spirit. An example of this kind would be the shedding of tears of love, of gratitude, of devotion, of longing, and of joy.

These touching emotions (and the consequent shedding of tears) are experienced when their author finds himself face-to-face with events which, though not exclusively joyful in content, are still, in some way or other, capable of evoking concepts and memories tinged with sadness.

Only in heaven, where joy is pure and unalloyed, will God dry every tear from the eyes of the blessed (see Apoc 21:4); yet, even on this earth, holy sorrow always brings its meed of comfort.

The value and significance of tears must be judged by the occasion causing them, that is, according to the parallel emotions they evoke.

Whereas "the sorrow of the world" evokes sinful tears, the "sorrow that is according to God" sheds blessed tears (2 Cor 7:10).

The children of this world sorrow in a sinful, or at most only in a natural, fashion and hence shed impassioned tears when their lusts are not satisfied. They can expect no comfort from the Holy Spirit.

The children of God, on the contrary, sorrow and weep in a virtuous manner and consequently, in their woe and misery, they are comforted by the Holy Spirit.

Manifold are the grounds and occasions afforded us in this vale of tears for sorrow according to God's good pleasure. In virtue of our native weakness, we are permitted to mourn and weep even over earthly needs and temporal miseries, but with due Christian resignation.

Still, animated by a holy love and sorrow, we should, above all, weep over our sins and imperfections, over the danger of sinning and of thus ultimately losing our soul eternally.

In addition, we should weep over the sins of others, over the numberless offenses against the Majesty of God, over the perdition and eternal damnation of so many souls purchased by the blood of Christ, over the incessant oppressions, persecutions, and slanders against the Church, over the Passion of Christ, over the dolors of the Blessed Mother of God, over the torments of the poor souls, over the prolongation of our pilgrimage from the face of God and our heavenly home.

These are genuine tears that are shed before the Lord (*Ploremus coram Domino*—Ps 94:6) that is, tears inspired by the Holy Spirit and hence are not only holy and salutary but also comforting. So, for example, tears of compunction are at first bitter (*Petrus flevit amare*—"Peter wept bitterly"—Lk 22:62), but soon they are sweetened by the Holy Spirit Who removes all anxiety and tribulation from the soul, and, in its stead, instills peace and quiet because it has again been reconciled to God. The saints are on record as testifying from personal experience that no comfort is more precious here below than tears elicited out of love and devotion.

Scripture and the liturgy often recommend prayer with tears, for these lend to our petitions a special great power and efficacy.

Tobias prayed with tears (see Tb 12:12) and the angel presented his prayer to the Lord. "I have heard thy prayer, and I have seen thy tears" was the Lord's announcement to King Ezechias and "[He added to his] days fifteen years" (Is 38:5).

We can form a fair estimate of the value and blessing of tears from the fact that with hardly any other unusual grace has God, in His goodness, been so lavish as in the bestowal of the wonderful gift of pious tears. Our missal also contains a powerful prayer petitioning for the grace of wholesome tears of penance and compunction.

The Church offers the eucharistic sacrifice to the divine Majesty so that, through the bestowal of the grace of the Holy Spirit, He may draw tears of compunction from our stony hearts and elicit from our eyes a flood of tears (*lacrimarum flumina*).

Thus, through our weeping, we will wash away the stains of our sins and extinguish the enkindled flames that we have deserved.[36] In the wake of forgiven sin, there succeeds the blissful consciousness of being once again a free, happy child of God.

After crying and weeping, the Holy Spirit pours in joyfulness (see Tb 3:22).

After sorrow comes joy; after the storm, the calm. But the Holy Spirit gladdens the sorrowful heart not only through the drying of his tears but also by making those very tears serve as an element of consolation.

Tears are thus a source of refreshment in grief, while weeping relieves the soul bent down with sorrow and depressed with trouble.

"Dare I ask, O Lord, why it is that the tears shed by the unhappy soul benefit him?

"Or hast Thou cast away our misery far from Thee?

"Eternally, You repose peacefully in Yourself, while we are tossed about by divers trials.

"And yet, unless we mourned in Thine ears, we should have no remnant of hope left us.

"Whence, then, is sweet fruit gathered from the bitterness of life, from groaning, tears, and complaints?

"Does this sweeten it that we hope Thou hearest?

"This is true of prayer, for therein is a longing to approach unto Thee."[37]

The keener the sorrow, the more copiously does He allow the tears to well forth until they mantle the face like the dew of the morning.

But my words can in no wise brush them aside. Even though I were endowed with this power, yet would I restrain it, because, in moments of deep emotion, it is a blessing to be able to weep.

Says St. Ambrose: "In the dew of tears, deep sorrow expires."[38]

Let us, therefore, with frequent earnestness, invoke the Holy Spirit to come to our aid in all the trials of life and to help us shed no other but only pious and salutary tears.

Third Stanza (Literal Translation)

O most blessed Light.
Fill Thou the inmost recesses of the hearts of Thy faithful!
Without Thy divine assistance,
there is nothing in man, nothing harmless.

Both by its position and by its contents, this stanza forms an apt connecting link and transition between the preceding and the following stanzas. If the invocations up to this point have been spoken with upright mind and in a recollected spirit, then the concept of the Holy Spirit's infinite goodness and His immeasurable treasures of grace must have dawned more vividly upon the pious man of prayer, together with a more pronounced consciousness of his own indigence and helplessness.

Such a disposition is expressed in the next six verses:

O lux beatissima,
Reple cordis intima,
Tuorum fidelium.
(Light of heav'nly blessedness,
Banish sin's black wretchedness,
Share with us Thy happiness.)

"*O most blessed Light.*"—This is the outcry of adoring wonder and praise of the Holy Spirit Who eternally proceeds from the Father and the Son as an immortal shining Stream of Fire, as the uncreated Plenitude of love and joy.

O *Beata Trinitas*—"O Blessed Trinity"—so the Church, in a burst of childlike, jubilant love prays and sings, again and again, on Trinity Sunday; for in face of this profound, unfathomable mystery, all other words seem, as it were, to die on her lips.

The Holy Spirit is called "blessed Light" because, as Love, He lays claim to a blessed life in an infinite degree, and because, out of the boundless plenitude of His own Blessedness, every other type of blessedness pours forth that is found in the world of angels and of men. He, in a very special way, is Love (see 1 Jn 4:8), and this Love is infinitely enjoyable, delightful, blissful in itself, and renders all creatures blissful.

While we in deep awe direct our gaze upward to the Holy Spirit, the spontaneous wish and desire is awakened that He may replenish us in copious measure with the delightful riches of His light and warmth. We request the fullness of heavenly understanding, love, and joy.

With this heaped-up measure of His good gifts, the Holy Spirit satisfies, stills, and sates our longing as far as it is possible in this life (see Ps 102:5).

The petition further asks that "the most blessed Light" of the Holy Spirit may radiate and inflame the inmost and deepest recesses (*cordis intima*) of our hearts. Adduced as motive for hearing this request is the fact that through a well-grounded and living faith we are linked by peculiar ties of dependence and possession to the Holy Spirit (*tuorum fidelium*).

Through the Sacraments of Baptism and Confirmation, we are quite completely His, and hence we should belong to Him exclusively.

Faith alone reveals to the mind the greatness, the worth, and the glory of grace, and faith alone impels the will to seek and to preserve this heavenly treasure of grace. With firm, unshaken faith in the power and goodness of the Holy Spirit, we cry out accordingly:

"O Thou everlasting Light, surpassing all created lights, dart the beams of Thy brightness from above to penetrate all the inmost recesses of my heart. Purify, rejoice, enlighten, and quicken my spirit and all its powers, that I may cleave unto Thee with superabounding, triumphant joy.

"Oh, when will that blessed and desired hour come, that Thou mayest satisfy me with Thy presence and mayest be unto me All in all? So long as this is not granted me, I shall not have perfect joy."[39]

Such plenitude of the Holy Spirit is, above all, essential for those called to work for the sanctification of their neighbor.

They must be so rich in the treasures of wisdom and virtue that they may always be able to share their spiritual abundance with others.

The daily cultivation of the interior life is, therefore, indispensable to the priest in the blessed administration of his pastoral office.

The contemplative life must ever serve as the spring and guiding star of the active life.

The spiritual director must be upright in intention, above reproach in his conduct, prudent in the observance of silence, edifying in his speech, a neighbor to all by sympathetic charity, and, above all, a man given to meditation and contemplation.

As his solicitude for the interior life should not act as a barrier to the management of external affairs, so neither should his concern with outside matters be an obstacle to his zeal for his own interior.[40]

Our earnest petitions are founded on the absolute poverty and inability of man with reference to his supernatural, eternal salvation, his heavenly destiny.

Sine tuo numine[41]
Nihil est in homine,
Nihil est innoxium.
(Lo, without Thy breath divine
Holiness nowhere can shine,
No man ever can be Thine.)

Man's end, his eternal destiny to enjoy the unimpeded, direct Beatific Vision of God is supernatural, that is, it surpasses the exigencies and powers not only of human nature but of all created nature in general. Life on this earth furnishes the preparation, the highway, to this heavenly glory and happiness, and so even these preliminary steps must be essentially supernatural in character. Only a supernatural life is conducive to the pursuit and attainment of eternal salvation. Now by nature man has nothing and can do absolutely nothing that will bring him nearer to this high and exalted goal.

In the business of salvation, man depends entirely on the merciful operation and sway of the Holy Spirit. Even "the beginning of our salvation," the very first step up the steep slopes of the Christian, that is, the supernatural life—our holy Catholic Faith—must be accounted a very precious, a priceless gift of heaven. (*Coeleste fidei donum*—so the Vatican Council.)

When God imparts to us the grace of faith through the Sacrament of Baptism together with the shining garment of innocence and the bright adornment of all the supernatural virtues, He calls us into His marvelous light (see 1 Pt 2:9).

The marvelous light of faith affords joy to the children of God, even on their earthly pilgrimage, and leads them in the next world to the full possession of perfect happiness in their eternal heavenly home.

Our own holy Faith even teaches us that "every cloud, no matter how threatening, has its sunny side turned heavenward."[42]

We even grant that man, with his natural powers, can learn many a truth and perform many a deed of natural virtue, but he is incapable of his own power to wage a continuously successful warfare against evil concupiscence, to overcome all temptations, and to obey the moral law in its entirety. For his higher, supernatural destiny he can accomplish absolutely nothing.

The very first advance toward holiness does not proceed from the will of man but from the supernatural impulse of God.

Without the benign and powerful guidance and operation of the Holy Spirit (*numen*), without interior enlightenment and inspiration from above, the soul is devoid of the least salutary thought or holy resolve. Man of himself possesses nothing profitable to salvation, nothing that is conducive to eternal happiness.

"No man can say The Lord Jesus, but by the Holy Ghost" (1 Cor 12:3), that means no one, without the supernatural influence of the Holy Spirit, can invoke the name of Jesus in a manner that is profitable for salvation.[43] Without the help of grace, man can do nothing (see Jn 15:5), that is, he can perform no work whatsoever that is profitable or meritorious. Divine grace, supernatural help, and the support of the Holy Spirit are, accordingly, indispensable if we are to tread the pathway of salvation, continue on the same, and happily arrive at its end.

Step-by-step, then, the Holy Spirit must enlighten and guide the pilgrim to his heavenly home, strengthen and protect him, lest he stray from the path and come to grief.

May Thy grace, therefore, O Lord, ever anticipate us, accompany us, and constrain us ever to the zealous pursuance of good works.

From the Holy Spirit proceed all salutary thoughts, inspirations, and counsels, all pious impulses and consolations, all holy resolutions and deeds of piety.[44]

Just as without the operation of the Holy Spirit, there is nothing supernaturally good in man (*Nihil est in homine*) so, too, without His grace, there is nothing pure, flawless, or faultless (*Nihil est innoxium*).

A special efficacy is added by the repetition of the little word *nihil* (nothing). Only the grace of the Holy Spirit can free the soul from sin, and preserve it without stain.

Innocence and purity in thought and action blossom and thrive only under the sweet and powerful touch of the divine Spirit.

Without grace, we can do absolutely nothing (see Jn 15:5)—this should make us humble; with His grace which strengthens us, we can do all things (see Phil 4:13)—this thought should make us magnanimous. These two virtues, humility and magnanimity, must always go hand in hand.

Fourth Stanza (Literal Translation)

Cleanse what is stained,
Bedew what is parched,
Heal what is wounded;
Bend what is rigid,
Warm what is chilled,
Guide what is astray.

What is more repulsive than vileness and filth? Hence, this picture is especially apt to inculcate a horror for sin. Sin defiles the soul. In a very special way, impurity sullies soul and body. Only a soul supernaturally enlightened can in any way or in the smallest degree surmise how hateful and loathsome sin must be in the eyes of the all-Holy God, in Whose sight the heavens are not pure. As the soul in the state of grace is unspeakably beautiful and lovely and resplendent, so, through sin, that soul is rendered foul and repulsive. Hence, from this first and most formidable evil, we pray to be delivered.

Who can make pure the impure? The Holy Spirit alone (see Jb 14:4), He alone it is that blots out iniquities (see Is 43:25) and forgives all sins. This cleansing action is frequently stressed in the liturgy and often ascribed to the fire of the Holy Spirit. Here, in this instance, another metaphor is employed, since it is now a question of "washing away impurities." Water is the most appropriate element for washing, and, as such, it is meant here insofar as it symbolizes, in a splendid manner, the sin-destroying power of grace, and in the Sacrament of Baptism is particularly efficacious in purifying the soul from sin. Since all grace and the efficacy of the means of grace were merited through the sacrificial death of

Christ on the Cross, the purification from sin is also ascribed to the sacrificial blood of Christ, that is, to the shedding of His blood.

The blood of Jesus Christ, of the Son of God, cleanses us from all sin (see 1 Jn 1:7), for Christ loved us and cleansed us from our sins in His own blood (see Apoc 1:5).

Hence blessed are they who wash their robes in the blood of the Lamb (see Apoc 22:14). But while the blood of Christ frees from sin indirectly, (as the source of satisfaction and merit), divine grace directly removes all sinfulness from the soul.

Thus we pray that the Holy Spirit, through the heavenly water of His grace, may wash away from the soul every defilement until it is rendered clean and spotless.

The word *lava* (wash, clean) characterizes the cleaning as an inward effect, for it signifies that the defilement of sin is not merely covered over but is actually taken away, that is, it is blotted out, destroyed, annihilated. Everything sinful is completely removed and entirely disappears even in the sight of God. The limpid, life-giving waters of the Holy Spirit enjoy, in addition, the wonderful power of not merely freeing the soul from sin, but endowing her at the same time with an unearthly splendor and a supernatural beauty. A soul, just a moment before marred by the ravages of sin, is in the flash of an eye made purer, brighter, more dazzling than the freshly fallen snow: "Thou shalt wash me, and I shall be made whiter than snow" (Ps 50:9).

In the exact degree of a man's advance in the practical knowledge of heavenly things and in the interior life, will his awareness of guilt become more acute and his conscience more sensitive. For this very reason, the perfect never cease to pray: "Wash me yet more from my iniquity" (Ps 50:4).

Venial sins, even imperfections, more or less, dim the shining luster of the garment of grace. From these, the pilgrim of earth, in his contact with the dust and worldly associations, can never fully emancipate himself. Consequently, the radical, thorough cleansing of the heart ever remains not only the first but also the persistent task and occupation of the spiritual life. To effect this purity, the soul must freely mingle her tears of compunction and love with the waters of salvation, with the stream of our Redeemer's grace, which issue forth from the Savior's pierced side and spring up into life everlasting (see Jn 4:14).

As in the physical world, the element water is accorded a prominent place, so also in the spiritual order and in Holy Scripture. In virtue of its properties, it is a perfect symbol of divine grace and its manifold activities. As it cleanses what is foul, so it imparts to the parched earth the moisture necessary for the growth of plant life. With this function of water uppermost in mind, the Church has us cry out to the Holy Spirit:

Riga quod est aridum
(Bedew what is parched)

What fresh water, rain, and the dew of the heavens are to the parched, thirsting soil, that the living water, which the Holy Spirit draws from the fountains of the Savior (see Is 12:3) and imparts to the faithful, is for the soul.

Water calls forth life, promotes growth and fruitfulness in the world of nature. A well-watered garden or plot of ground is productive. When the Lord visits the land and waters it, He insures a generous harvest. He sends down His showers to moisten the furrows and fructifies the tender shoots, so that the crops refreshed with the warm rains may yield plentiful returns. The meadows blossom forth in rich opulence. The beautiful places of the wilderness sparkle with green, while the hills are girded about with joy and the vales abound with corn (see Ps 64:10–14).

This blessing of nature, this fruitfulness of the land, is a symbol of the rich, liberal harvest which the Holy Spirit calls forth and brings to fruitage in the spiritual fields of the Church, through the heavenly dew of His grace (see 1 Cor 3:9).

From the Holy Spirit, as the exuberant Fountainhead of life, flow rivers of living water (see Jn 7:38) which vivify the soul, that it may bear much fruit (see Jn 15:5).

From the very first Pentecost, "the showers of gracious gifts, the streams of blessings, have watered every desert and all the dry land, for the Spirit of God 'moved over the waters' to renew the face of the earth, and, to drive away the old darkness. Flashes of new light shone forth, when by the blaze of those fiery tongues was kindled the Lord's bright word and fervent eloquence, in which there lay both a capacity of enlightening the mind and a power of consuming the rust of sin."[45]

"Having become a temple of the Holy Spirit and more than ever filled to overflowing with the stream of divine grace, we must not allow ourselves to be overcome by any immoderate desire or ruled by any passion, lest the dwelling of virtue and sanctity be polluted."[46]

The influence of the Holy Spirit upon the life of grace is presented here in a figurative sense, as the drenching of the soul with heavenly dew and rain. But, whereas, in the case of plant life, water only assists and promotes its growth, the influence of the Holy Spirit, in the case of the soul, is quite otherwise.

The salutary waters of grace, streaming forth from Him, fructify the soul in a supernatural manner, that nobler heavenly fruits may be produced. This picture points, at the same time, to the necessity of grace.

The earth and the soil are unproductive save with water. In parallel manner, the human soul is barren of supernatural life and fruitfulness unless it be watered by the fount of graces emanating from the Holy Spirit.

It is a severe punishment when the Lord closes the heavens and commands the clouds to let no rain fall upon the vineyard (see Is 5:6). But incomparably more tragic is the punishment meted out by the Holy Spirit upon unrepented sin in withholding or diminishing the rich flood of His stream of graces. As a consequence, and due to their own fault, such souls are gradually impoverished and finally perish miserably. Bereft of the waters of salvation and of the Holy Spirit, man is like a branch separated from the vine which dries up and is cast into the fire (see Jn 15:6). "Deign, therefore, to shower Thy grace from above and my heart will be steeped in this heavenly dew! Supply fresh waters of devotion to irrigate the face of the earth, to bring forth good and perfect fruit."[47] As water is life-giving and productive of fruit, so it also provides refreshment and comfort (see Ps 22:2), especially in slaking thirst. Hence this verse concludes with the petition that the Holy Spirit may accord us the grace of devotion and His strengthening consolations. For "without grace what am I but a withered branch and a useless trunk, meet only to be cast away?"[48] A plot of dried up farm land that is neither watered by a brook, nor moistened by the rain and dew of heaven, suggests the state of soul that is visited with spiritual dryness or aridity. In such an oppressive, melancholy frame of mind, one feels abandoned by God, because he is without palpable devotion, without joy or perception for divine things, or a sense of delight and enthusiasm in the service of God. Spiritual aridity of this sort, especially when it is undeserved, should tend to purify a soul more and more from all manifestations of self-love, even the most petty and most hidden; it should incite to the practice of humility and patience, and to heroic immolation of self. But alas, only too often are we so painfully aware of our spiritual aridity that we may well pray the Holy Spirit to restore to us again the joy and delight of His salvation, the unspeakably blessed perception of His presence (see Ps 50:14) by comforting and refreshing our withered and fainting heart with the sweet heavenly dews of His consolations. "If thou hast not devotion but rather findest thyself dry, persist in prayer, sigh, and knock; nor desist until thou deservest to receive some crumb or drop of this saving precious grace."[49]

"Cleanse what is stained; bedew what is parched."—These two petitions bear directly on the soul's interior progress; the heart must, first of all, be purified, since only a pure heart can bring forth good fruit and taste the joy of true devotion. Thus the heavenly husbandman "cleanses every branch that bears fruit that it may bear more fruit" (see Jn 15:2), that is, He purifies the soul of all obnoxious growths and of all inordinate attachment to temporal things, that it may be enriched in its Christian outlook and life. Through works of mortification and mercy, we should take pains "to be set free from the filth of sin and to become rich in the fruits of love."[50]

"May the outpouring of the Holy Spirit purify our hearts, O Lord, and, by the inward sprinkling of heavenly dew, may they be made fruitful"—in this strain the Church prays accordingly on the feast of Pentecost.

In order that our soul may always be purified, quickened, and refreshed by the heavenly waters of grace of the Holy Spirit, we must zealously cultivate the spirit of prayer, perform all our pious exercises of devotion punctually and attentively, for the prophet compares the man meditating day and night on the law of the Lord to a tree which is planted near the running waters, whose leaf shall not fall off, and which shall bring forth its fruit in season (see Ps 1:2–3).

Sana quod est saucium.
(Heal what is wounded.)

Theologically, this verse speaks volumes. Hence this picture (the healing of wounded mankind) is used with special predilection to denote the work of our redemption accomplished by Christ and completed in each individual soul by the Holy Spirit through participation in the means of salvation won for us by Christ.

In consequence of the defection of our first parents, as well as through personal sin, the human race has been mortally wounded and is therefore seriously sick. It can only be healed and restored to perfect health through the heavenly medicine of the blood of Christ in virtue of the redemptive graces dispensed by the Holy Spirit.

Inasmuch as Jesus Christ cures mankind from sin and its consequences, He is, in truth, the Savior of the world (see Jn 4:42).

Through the bloody, painful wounds of our divine Savior, we are healed of the grievous wounds that sin inflicted upon us (see 1 Pt 2:24). As the heavenly Physician, the Holy Spirit continuously pours into the wounds of fallen mankind (see Lk 10:34) the wine of Jesus Christ's sacrificial blood and the oil of His healing grace, that "eternal health of soul and body" may come to it.

But, strictly speaking, weakness and concupiscence inherent in human nature can rightly be designated a wounding, only inasmuch as they are actually occasioned by sin.

Original Sin destroyed the supernatural health, conferred on the human race at the dawn of history, and thus inflicted mortal wounds on human nature. These wounds—the darkening of the understanding, the tendency of the will to evil, concupiscence, and the weakness of the flesh—are aggravated by personal sin. Only the baneful effects and corrupting consequences of sin, which in part remain in man even when sin itself has been destroyed, may, properly speaking, be understood by wounds and sickness of the soul. In the wider sense of the word, however, sin itself is implied as far as it continues in the soul until it is repented of and forgiven.

If we understand the wounding of the soul, endowed with supernatural gifts and privileges, in this wider sense of the term, then it becomes clear at once that for the complete cure, that is, for the restoration of its impaired health, both sanctifying and actual grace are needed.

Actual grace, because of its twofold function, is generally regarded as "healing" and "elevating."

It is called "healing" grace insofar as it assists our moral weakness and strengthens frail nature in the overcoming of existing difficulties.

It is called "elevating" grace insofar as it renders the natural powers of the soul inwardly capable of producing works supernatural in character and merit. It is to be noted, however, that both functions, as a rule, synchronize, that is, that one and the same grace heals and simultaneously works the sanctification of corrupted nature.

The petition for "the healing of the soul's wounds" includes, in fact presupposes, this supernatural, elevating action of grace, for the Holy Spirit supports our weakness by the supernatural help of His grace.

The fact that we ask here expressly only for the restoration of health to our diseased being, according to the direction of the Church, will appear all the more purposeful, the more keenly we perceive from actual experience that corrupt nature left to its own devices is ever prone to evil and to the things of earth, and, consequently, often plunges man into sin and perdition.

To judge of the gravity of our ailment, think only of the medicine which effects its cure. Contemplate the woeful figure of our suffering Lord, the shedding of Our Blessed Lord's blood on the Cross, and it will dawn on you how very precious a remedy the Redeemer has prepared in His blood for our wretched sinful state.

"Surely He hath borne our infirmities and carried our sorrows....

"But He was wounded for our iniquities, He was bruised for our sins: the chastisement of our peace was upon Him, and by His bruises we are healed" (Is 53:4–5).

Accordingly, it will cost us not a few sacrifices to free ourselves, little by little, from all the maladies, infirmities, and passions of the soul. The generous practice of self-denial possesses, in a superlative degree, the healing power that is demanded for a radical cure.

Not only "oil" but also "wine" must be poured into the wounds (see Lk 10:34). We must not recoil from a medicine that is bitter and galling. What do men not seldom brave and endure in order to restore health to their mortal, perishable bodies! Should we be less concerned in restoring and preserving the health of our immortal soul?

"After lusting flesh has been overcome by the strivings of the spirit (see Gal 5:17), man is in possession of free health and healthy freedom, so that the flesh is ruled by the decision of the spirit and the spirit by the help of God's graces."[51]

As a "living Fountain," the Holy Spirit purifies us in the bath of Baptism and of Penance.

As "the spiritual Unction," He heals the wounds of our evil tendencies and of our fatal weakness, primarily in the Sacrament of Extreme Unction, which was instituted to restore perfect health and healing in grave illness that threatens to destroy life.

The two figurative expressions, "Cleanse what is stained" and "Heal what is wounded," supplement and clarify each other. The first refers more to the guilt of sin; the second, chiefly to the remains, the consequences of sin. For the alleviation of an illness that is difficult to cure and only too often defies a cure, we now pray in the following verse:

Flecte quod est rigidum
(Bend what is rigid)

Man is not constrained by divine grace to do good, but retains his full liberty. He is free, therefore, to resist the Holy Spirit and His grace; in a word, he can spurn the graces offered him for his eternal salvation.

Resistance to the operations of the Holy Spirit must bring in its wake the most fearful consequences and draw down severe punishments upon itself. Through sin, that is, through neglect, abuse, or contempt of grace, man's receptiveness for the successful operations of grace is diminished. At the same time, he handicaps himself in the use and cooperation of grace.

If a soul sets an obstacle to the reception and free let of grace, God, as a rule, punishes such ingratitude by stemming the rich flow of graces He was thus far wont to give. Thus, reason and judgment, in reference to the supernatural, are more and more clouded, resulting ultimately in spiritual darkness and hardness of heart. Both often lead to final impenitence and eternal perdition.

Sins and passions, therefore, harden the heart, that is, render it impervious to higher things and insensible to wholesome influences, from whatever quarter they may come.

The conversion of a blinded and hardened heart is uncommonly difficult, because an unusual measure of interior illuminations and inspirations are necessary in order to soften or move it to such an extent that a man may work out his salvation "with fear and trembling" (Phil 2:12). Such a generous measure of graces, however, is a very special and, hence, a very rare, manifestation of God's mercy. For this type of grace we here pray when we beg the Holy Spirit to mollify the sulky mind and to move the recalcitrant will to good, and to render the rebellious heart docile and responsive to wholesome instruction and admonition.

"As the divisions of waters, so the heart of the king is in the hand of the Lord: whithersoever He will, He shall turn it" (Prv 21:1).

God's treasures of grace being infinite, He can, in His divine omnipotence, transform interiorly the most hardened of hearts.

Already in the Old Testament, He promised to give us a new heart and to put a new spirit within us; to take away the stony heart and give us a heart of flesh (see Ez 36:26). This hardness of heart is overcome by the Holy Spirit Who copiously beams down His splendid rays upon the soul and awakens and fosters holy sentiments of fear, compunction, hope, and love.

This petition is so flexible in interpretation that it applies likewise to the condition of those souls who, not through mortal sin to be sure, but, through venial sin, guiltily deprive themselves of many heavenly graces and favors and become less receptive and docile to the inner guidance of the Holy Spirit. For if one too often gratifies his natural inclinations, is too yielding to sensual and worldly attachments, pays no heed to higher inspirations, and resists the tuggings of grace, the heart very frequently becomes hardened in lukewarmness and imperfections. This unhealthy condition of soul is especially dangerous and its prevention is easier than its cure.

"To day if you shall hear His voice, harden not your hearts" (Ps 94:8), for "a hard heart shall fear evil at the last" (Ecclus 3:27).

Fove quod est frigidum
(Warm what is benumbed)

Here we call upon the Holy Spirit to arouse and foster in the lukewarm burning zeal, flaming devotion, and enthusiasm. Now, though no two things seem so incompatible as fire and water, still both symbolize the Holy Spirit and His operations. He is not only a cleansing, fructifying, and refreshing Spring of life (*fons vivus*) but also a flaming River of fire (*fluvius igneus*).

The word *fovere*, moreover, connotes, above all, not so much fire itself as the transmitting of one's own bodily warmth.

The Holy Spirit is the Love of God in a Person and so, true to His nature, He takes all rational creatures under His wing and nourishes and sustains them by the infusion of His own divine life. This spiritual warmth consists substantially in the supernatural love of God and neighbor, and so we ask here, preeminently, for the bestowal and increase of this theological virtue. Where the heavenly fire of love has been extinguished, there coldness and death hold sway; but where, on the contrary, it flames and burns vigorously, there the heart is all aglow with heavenly zeal and ever charged with streams of fresh eternal life.

No mere human being can fully grasp and adequately express how precious, sweet, and delightful is charity, the highest gift of God and the greatest of the virtues (see 1 Cor 13:13). Its possessor is a child of God and a hallowed, and beautifully adorned temple of the Holy Spirit; for wherever love takes up its abode in the soul, there also the Holy Spirit dwells with His grace, His seven gifts, and all the virtues.

Love is the root from which the other virtues spring.

Love is the bond of perfection (see Col 3:14) insofar as it comprises all the other virtues and binds them together into one harmonious whole.

Love is the soul of all the virtues and pious acts, since love completes and quickens them, that is, renders them pleasing to

God and meritorious of heavenly reward. Thus love is the zenith and crown of all Christian virtues, the power and marrow of all virtuous striving and meritorious effort. Love is, therefore, something sublime.

"Nothing is sweeter than love, nothing stronger, nothing higher; nothing more pleasant, nothing fuller in heaven or in earth; for love is born of God and cannot rest but in God above all created things. Love often knoweth no measure but groweth fervent above all measure.

"When weary it is not tired.

"Like a vivid flame and a burning torch it mounteth upward and securely passeth through all."[52]

How solicitously we should guard and nurture this holy, heavenly, divine, and blessed fire in our hearts!

Fire, by its nature, is always flickering and restless. The same is true of love, ever constraining us to pray, to work, to fight, to suffer, to make sacrifices for God's Kingdom and the salvation of souls. On the other hand, how unworthy, how saddening, how dangerous is coldness, lukewarmness, and indifference in God's service.

"Because iniquity hath abounded the charity of many shall grow cold" (Mt 24:12), says our Lord.

Divine love, true and lofty, is weakened and finally stifled when false, poisonous, and sinful love of the world entangles and ensnares the heart. Against this danger we must arm and protect ourselves through self-denial, and mortification, as well as by meditation and prayer to the Holy Spirit, Who, as a pent-up Furnace of divine Love, can inflame our hearts ever anew to fresh, vigorous zeal.

"Our fervor and progress ought to increase daily; but now it is esteemed a great thing if anyone can retain something of his first fervor."[53] To many a man, therefore, may be applied the warning of the Holy Ghost: "But I have somewhat against thee, that thou hast left thy first charity. Be mindful therefore from whence thou art fallen: and do penance and do the first works" (Apoc 2:4–5).

And if you should fail to realize your own lukewarmness but imagine yourself to be "rich and made wealthy" and having "need of nothing," then indeed you are "wretched and miserable and poor and blind and naked" (Apoc 3:17), and there is every reason to resume your former fervor and apply yourself to penance and instant prayer, begging the Holy Spirit to inflame your heart anew.

Rege quod est devium.
(Guide what is astray.)

Guide and direct to the way of salvation, all that has gone astray.

To the Holy Spirit is ascribed the work of enlivening, moving, and guiding all things, more especially man in the supernatural order and with reference to his supernatural end.

He is the Guide, par excellence, of the interior life of the spirit. Through His grace we are made capable of comprehending, and of embracing with love, what is supernaturally true and good. He directs us to the practice of every virtue and guides our steps on the road of peace. Christian truth and teaching is the divinely designated path, the norm, revealed by God for man's religious moral life, and, as such, is styled in Scripture, "the way" (see Acts 9:2). This designation is more clearly stamped in those texts where Christianity is called "the way of God" (see Acts 18:26), and "the way of the Lord" (Acts 18:25), "the way of truth" (2 Pt 2:2), and "of justice" (2 Pt 2:21), "the way of salvation" (Acts 16:17). This way was revealed and opened to us by God in Christ, and, therefore, it is truth in the absolute. It establishes us in proper supernatural relationship with God and leads us to eternal salvation.

Christianity is the only true way, that is, the one correct norm, for the religious thought and upright conduct of man. All who travel this right way (see 2 Pt 2:15) reach the heavenly homeland. But the one who forsakes this way and ambles off from the same, stumbles upon crooked paths and deceptive lanes that eventually lead to the abyss of eternal perdition. Knowledge of Christ's teaching as well as observance of Christ's commandments and counsels is the "narrow way" of salvation that leads to life and happiness, but which "few find and choose." The spurning of His teaching and His law is the "broad road" that leads to destruction and "many there are who enter that way" (see Mt 7:13–14).

The pathway of virtue is only at first narrow and difficult, but, as one advances, it becomes ever more beautiful, peaceful, and charming (see Prv 3:17) the more the Holy Spirit, through the light of His grace, dilates the heart with love and joy. Those whose hearts are all aglow with divine love and filled with spiritual joy do not plod along, but joyfully run the way of salvation with its sacrificial demands.

Joy is an effect of love and both these are fruits of the Holy Spirit (see Ps 118:32).

The consciousness of our weakness constrains us to proffer the petition that the Holy Spirit may ever graciously deflect whatever would decoy us from the only true way and from our ultimate goal.

"All we like sheep have gone astray, every one hath turned aside into his own way" (Is 53:6), hence the necessity to call upon the Holy Spirit ever and anon to show us His ways and to teach us His paths (see Ps 24:4).

The guidance of the Holy Spirit is both sweet and mighty (see Ws 8:1), for He gives not only delight and joy but also supplies strength and courage to enable us to persevere on the pathway of virtue (see Ecclus 24:25).

He offers protection in all dangers that beset the pathway of salvation. He sees to it that no insurmountable obstacles obstruct the progress of piety or hinder the attainment of our last end. He ever revives and refreshes, consoles and strengthens the weary pilgrim until he reaches the heavenly homeland.

In the Church, the Holy Spirit has "so beneficially transformed men who had trod evil and corrupt ways that they no longer, as is the wont of the children of the world, center their thoughts upon the earthly but, as if sprung from heaven, busy themselves with a far nobler good."[54]

Fifth Stanza (Literal Translation)

Give to Thy faithful confiding in Thee
Thy sevenfold gifts,[55]
Give them the reward of virtue;
Give them the death of safety (a happy death),
Give them eternal joy.

The humble insistent petitions for the manifold gifts and graces have increased our longing in the highest degree. In this attitude of mind, we now sum up once more in the concluding verses all our pleas, imploring of the Holy Spirit the sum total of goods, the most precious, which He can confer for time and for eternity.

The fact that the four verses (even as the six that have immediately preceded) are set side by side without any connectives adds power and intensity to this supplication.[56]

Da tuis fidelibus,
In te confidentibus,
Sacrum septenarium.
(Grant them who believingly
Place their confidence in Thee
Sev'nfold grace of sanctity.)

Among the requisites for a good prayer of petition, faith and trust easily rank first. The petitions must spring from faith as the root and find nourishment and support in unshaken trust. Such a prayer, strong in faith and full of trust, the Lord has assured us will be heard: "All things, whatsoever you ask when ye pray, believe that you shall receive: and they shall come unto you" (Mk 11:24).

"Be of good heart, daughter, thy faith hath made thee whole" (Mt 9:22). Hence, the power and efficacy of prayer rest primarily upon an unfaltering trust, for the simple reason that such trust, on the one hand, implies the glorification of the infinite power, goodness, and faithfulness of God, and, on the other, deepens and increases the receptiveness of him who prays for these gifts. It is, therefore, advisable often to awaken and "stir up" this trust afresh by pondering upon the sources of Christian hope and by imploring of the Holy Spirit a disposition of prayer which will be pleasing to God. "Blessed are all they that trust in the Lord" (see Ps 2:13)—"in the Lord," namely, Who spoke through the prophet. "Open thy mouth wide, and I will fill it" (Ps 80:11). He who, with vivid yearning, seeks salvation and help will be enriched with all that is genuinely good. Doubt and distrust must be rigorously excluded from the heart when man (as is the case here) asks for spiritual gifts essential to salvation and which prayer alone can attain.

What here impels us so urgently is above all the longing for the so-called "seven gifts of the Holy Spirit."[57] The spirit of wisdom and understanding, of counsel, of fortitude, of knowledge and godliness, and the fear of the Lord, rests upon the Messiah (see Is 11:2–3), for these gifts were bestowed in all their fullness upon the humanity of Christ. Since they are necessary for the attainment of the supernatural end, for the salvation of the soul, they are infused at the same time as sanctifying grace and divine love. But whereas the virtues qualify us to work supernaturally and to live on that plane, the gifts incline us to be docile to the impulses and inspirations of the Holy Spirit. Through them, mind and will are readily disposed to cooperate fully with the supernatural promptings evoked by the Holy Spirit. The gifts serve to support the virtues and bring them to perfection. In order to perform meritorious deeds, we need constant incentives, and as the case may be, must be docile to the stirrings and inspirations of the Holy Spirit. In virtue of these higher inspirations, or through His gifts, the Holy Spirit qualifies and incites us to the free and even spontaneous exercise of the supernatural virtues, imparting to us at the same time His helping and healing influence.

Manifold indeed are the shortcomings and frailties that aggravate the life of virtue. These are removed by the operation of the Holy Spirit, Who by means of His gifts sharpens our intellect and fortifies our judgment, even as He purifies and strengthens our volitions and aspirations. Thus the gifts not only promote a greater facility in the practice of virtue, but they elevate man to a loftier pinnacle and degree in Christian perfection. They are even requisite for the ordinary Christian life, but their influence is manifested more brilliantly in the performance of extraordinary deeds. Like heavenly seedlets, these gifts nestle in the soil of the sanctified soul, but, to be brought to full fruition, they require, above all things, painstaking cultivation on the part of man. We must especially persevere in earnest prayer to the Holy Spirit, imploring Him to prosper and fructify their growth.

"Now, we have received not the spirit of this world, but the Spirit that is of God: that we may know the things that are given us from God" (1 Cor 2:12).

The world's outlook on life has no time for the Holy Spirit and His gifts. He who is steeped in the world of sense, in the things of the moment, is spiritually blind and "nearsighted," that is, he has no range of vision for the heavenly and the eternal, but is wholly enmeshed in earthly goods and in transitory pleasures. Only he who is endowed with the divine light of faith and with the gifts of the Holy Spirit can have a clear perception of "the mystery of the Kingdom of God" (Lk 8:10), of the comforting strength and beauty of Christianity, of the joy and glory of the Redemption, of the Church's rich treasury of truth and graces. But only then will the knowledge of God and of things divine be fruitful and truly enjoyable when one, "full of faith and of the Holy Ghost" (Acts 6:5), immerses himself with childlike humility and purity of heart in the contemplation of the rich treasures of revelation, in the wonderful ambit of truths and facts pertaining to salvation. Following fast on the petition for this precious "sevenfold treasure of the gifts of the Holy Spirit" comes the earnest prayer that He may give us "the reward of virtue."

Da virtutis meritum
(Grant us virtue's reward)

Only those acts of virtue, only those morally good works which are supernatural in every aspect, that is, performed in the state of grace, with the help of the Holy Spirit, and in virtue of a supernatural motive, are meritorious. Such meritorious deeds are the result of the mysterious cooperation of man's free will and of divine grace. They are truly ours and are, at the same time, the gifts of the divine mercy. They are essential unto salvation. The just man—in possession of sanctifying grace, the supernatural virtues and gifts of the Holy Spirit—is a child of God and has, as such, the right to the inheritance of heaven (see Rom 8:17). Still, God does not will to grant him the glory and happiness of heaven out of pure generosity but also out of justice as an earned reward. All who are in a position to do so must merit heaven by good deeds. As a living branch on the divine Vine, we must bring forth fruit by allowing ourselves to be led, under the guidance of the Holy Spirit, Who dwells in us, to the untiring practice of every virtue.[58]

Although we must accept divine grace and cooperate with it wholeheartedly to make meritorious acts possible for us, still without this grace we are incapable of performing even the smallest meritorious act. For this ever-continuous influx of grace we here pray by calling upon the Holy Spirit to give us "the reward of virtue."

The Holy Spirit bestows meritorious acts of virtue by enlightening and encouraging man, by filling him with joy and love in the pursuance of the good, by supporting and strengthening him in the performance of virtuous deeds. This request for a generous bestowal of actual graces will be fully answered if we do our part, that is, if we make good use both of the graces themselves and of the time assigned for the gaining of merit, so that all our works will be complete, and every day of our lives full of good works (see Ps 72:10).

The Holy Spirit Who infuses the supernatural life also moves and incites the children of God (see Rom 8:14) to lead a supernatural, that is, a godly, heavenly, spiritual life, and, during the span of their pilgrimage, to "go from virtue to virtue" (Ps 83:8), until they enter the "heavenly Sion" to partake of the blessed eternal vision of God's glory.

The Church prays that "God may direct our actions, that, in the name of His beloved Son, we may become rich in good works." Such works are spiritual offerings, well pleasing to God, and enjoy a supernatural value in His sight.

"His grace always anticipates us and accompanies us and renders us zealous for every good work."[59]

The supernatural disposition of mind and will, whence spring these meritorious works, have their origin in the Holy Spirit. The apostle encourages the faithful to generous and cheerful giving from religious motives (see 2 Cor 9:6–15). The harvest depends on the sowing. If the seed is scattered lovingly, and hence, abundantly, a generous, bountiful harvest may be expected from God's munificence. Man should dispense his benefits with cheerfulness, and joy for "God loveth a cheerful giver" (2 Cor 9:7). Carrying on with fidelity, zeal, and kindliness in the pursuit of our calling, and in manifesting kindness toward all the downtrodden, will insure for us a rich heavenly reward. Though countless be the good works of man, his eternal recompense for them will be wholly dependent upon his dying in the state of grace, that is, as a child of God. Hence, death in the state of grace, that is, final perseverance, is a special gift of God for which we must humbly and constantly pray.

Da salutis exitum
(Grant a death of hope and peace)

Death is here expressed as a "departure" and a happy death as a "departure of salvation," that is, a departure that leads one to perfect and eternal salvation. Death is the decisive "exit" from this world and from this life. The soul, namely, quits the body and the body quits the world. "For, we have not here a lasting city" (Heb 13:14). The world is not our home. Fragile is man's mortal clay and fickle is his day. Man's body is an unstable "tabernacle" and his existence a transient abiding in this tabernacle (see 2 Pt 1:13–14). Man's death is the vacating of this earthly, perishable tabernacle, and a good death is the joyful, triumphal "entrance" into the everlasting Kingdom of Jesus Christ (see 2 Pt 1:11). As strangers upon the earth and as pilgrims toward the glorious city of God (see Heb 12:22), we spend but a short fleeting span of time in this mortal body and in this life. Still, the solemn moment of our departure is veiled in the mantle of darkness. The year, the day, and the hour are hidden from us that we may always be watchful and pray for a happy death. The coming of death at the moment when we are prepared is a very signal token of divine favor, the most precious of all divine graces. This grace we cannot strictly merit but, through persevering prayer, we may hope to obtain it. Let us never cease, then, day in and day out, to beg and implore that the Holy Spirit may grant us such rich and effective graces at the moment of our death that we may fight the last battle well, keep the Faith, run the course successfully, and then receive the crown that is laid up for us (see 2 Tm 4:7).

"O Lord Jesus Christ grant that after death we may joyfully enter the portals of paradise."

"O Almighty and merciful God, refresh the soul that Thou hast created in order that, at the hour of death, it may be delivered to Thee by Thy holy angels, free from the stain of sin."

"Almighty God, strengthen us with the grace of Thy holy Sacraments in order that we may not, at the hour of our death, succumb to the enemy, but merit to pass over with the angels into life, and grant us there a place of refreshment, happiness, rest, and the brightness of light."

In these strains we should often and devoutly pray with the Church. A life rich in virtue and merit is the best preparation for death, and a good death is the stepping stone to a joyful and blissful life in heaven for all eternity.

Da perenne gaudium.
(Grant eternal joy.)

"*Unto Thy faithful confiding in Thee grant eternal joy.*"—In this cry of petition, which encompasses the very highest craving of the heart of man, the Sequence reaches its climax and is effectively brought to a close. All foregoing petitions had reference to the use of grace in time; but this one concerns itself specifically with eternity.

Creation, redemption, sanctification—in short, all the works of God—find their completion beyond in the crowning of us pilgrims of earth with everlasting happiness. Three acts make up that happiness: the immediate and direct vision of God, then a love correspondingly most perfect and intimate, and finally the enjoyment, that is the peace, springing from this vision and love.

Heaven is light, love, and joy. The direct vision of God enkindles the most ardent love, and from both these arises the most blissful of delights. Only then is all yearning, all pining of the heart of man fully satisfied, only then is man perfectly happy when he, in clear vision and rapturous love, enjoys the infinite truth, goodness, and beauty of God, never to lose Him for all eternity.

The reward in eternity which answers to the merits won by good works here below is called happiness, and this happiness is here appropriately termed "everlasting joy." In this joy, the vision and love of God are included or presupposed as in germ and so they are here once more prayed for. The concept, moreover, of "eternal joy" is especially apt to attract and to spur on the human heart to despise the world and to be solely intent upon the kingdom of heaven. All crave happiness and call joy itself the blissful life of heaven.

We pray, therefore, for this heavenly, transcendent, perfect joy, and, since this is unspeakably great, only one of its attributes, namely, its endless duration, is expressly mentioned. Everlastingness belongs essentially to happiness. Hence it is that the perpetual duration, the eternity of the reward in the other life, is often stressed with predilection in both the Holy Scripture and the liturgy. This future joy is a supernatural and perfect participation in the happiness proper to God, in the "joy of thy Lord" (Mt 25:21) Himself, and as such, is likewise, everlasting.

Heavenly joy is without end. In this quality, it is quite distinct from the short, fleeting, and transitory joys of earth. Neither is it subject to diminution or change, but endures in undiminished plenitude and freshness forever. Toward this superabounding joy which no man can take from us (see Jn 16:22) all our daily aspirations and strivings should tend. This joy alone can quite fully satisfy us with perfect bliss.

"And the redeemed of the Lord shall return, and shall come into Sion with praise, and everlasting joy shall be upon their heads: they shall obtain joy and gladness, and sorrow and mourning shall flee away" (Is 35:10). But, in order to reap a joyous harvest in the world beyond, we must here below sow in tears (see Ps 125:5), for only those will enter into the joys of their Lord, into the land of endless bliss, who on earth take up their cross daily and in this way, and this way only, follow Christ always.

In every earthly need, in all the sufferings and trials of life as well as of death, the Holy Spirit is our Consoler, our "Best Consoler." His role of Comforter, however, will attain its crowning glory and its consummation only in the glorious resurrection when He will "wipe away all tears from [the] eyes" of the elect (Apoc 7:17). With these tender, love-inspired words, the great prophet had already consoled the sorrowing ones of Sion (see Is 25:8). Twice we find the same expression repeated in the last book of Holy Scripture. "And death shall be no more. Nor mourning, nor crying, nor sorrow shall be any more, for the former things are passed away" (Apoc 21:4). The children of God "who are come out of the great tribulation.... shall no more hunger nor thirst: neither shall the sun fall on them, nor any heat. For the Lamb, which is in the midst of the throne, shall rule them and shall lead them to the fountains of the waters of life" (Apoc 7: 14, 16–17). "And He that sat on the throne, said: Behold, I make all things new" (Apoc 21:5).

The new creation to emerge from the ruins of the world-conflagration will shine forth in supernatural, imperishable, heavenly splendor and beauty. Therefore, according to the promises of God (see Is 65:17; and 66:22), we await with intense desire and with absolute certainty, "new heavens and a new earth" (2 Pt 3:13). Here in the heavenly Jerusalem the children of God, with body and soul transfigured and glorified, shall find their happy eternal home.

"Joy and gladness shall be found therein, thanksgiving, and the voice of praise" (Is 51:3).

In the tones of "the eternal Alleluias," the songs of triumph and the heartfelt joy and gratitude of humankind redeemed from sin and death find expression. Jubilant strains of thankfulness will there prevail in recognition of the power and benignity with which the triune God dowered them on earth, and which, throughout eternity, will ever constitute for them a never-failing source of joy and bliss.

ENDNOTES

1 Whilst the coming into the hearts of the faithful is predicated of all the three Divine Persons, the fact of a sending is proper only to the Son and to the Holy Ghost. The Son comes indeed but as sent only by the Father; the Holy Ghost comes but as sent always and simultaneously by the Father and

the Son because He proceeds from both and is the Spirit of Them both. The act of being sent and of coming has always as objective the sanctification of man through the supernatural indwelling and action of the Holy Ghost.

2 *Tractates on the Gospel of John*, Tractate 76, no. 4.

3 Ignatius, *Spiritual Exercises*, Second Week.

4 The Holy Spirit comes from heaven and, since His descent does not involve a change of locale, He remains likewise in heaven, and from there He sends down His gifts to earth. Here then we ask for the light of the Holy Spirit—hence for a light that is spiritual, supernatural, and heavenly.

5 P. Wolter.

6 The first three verses furnish the theme of the whole hymn: the indwelling of the Holy Spirit and the communication of His treasures of grace.

7 Henry Suso.

8 See Teresa of Ávila, *Way of Perfection*, chap. 28.

9 Recall here the Knighthoods, Brotherhoods, and Hospitals of the Holy Spirit founded during the Ages of Faith. In the thirteenth century, Bavaria counted at least forty Hospitals of the Holy Spirit. See Emil Michael, S.J., *Kulturzustaende des Deutschen Volkes waehrend des 13. Jahrhunderts*, 2:181–255.

10 Very much to the point, in this connection, is the admonition found in the *Liturgical Year*, vol. 3, Paschal Time, for Thursday of Easter Week, issued by the Gothic Church of Spain to the faithful. "Dearly beloved brethren:... We should rejoice in that we have risen; but we should fear lest we may fall. We have been rescued from the death of old, and it behooves us to know how evil it was; we have been gifted with the new life, and we must cling to it as worthy of our love. To commit the sin we have been admonished to shun is not an error, but contempt. They that have been pardoned and relapsed deserve the greater punishment; nor is there excuse for them that have been once ransomed if they again become slaves."—Trans.

11 Both illuminating and astounding is the opinion of His Eminence, Cardinal Manning, who, himself crediting all the chief blessings and graces of his life for more than thirty years to the Holy Ghost devotion, once wrote: "I have long thought that the secret but real cause of the so-called Reformation was that the office of the Holy Ghost had been much obscured in popular belief." We can, therefore, do nothing better, more salutary, for our individual souls and the good of the Church at large, than by fervent recourse to the Holy Spirit to restore Him to the rightful position which He, as God, both deserves and merits in our views, in our lives, and in our devotions.—Trans.

12 Roman Breviary, Jan. 21.

13 *Oratio super populum*, of the Tuesday of Passiontide.

14 Henry Suso.

15 See Thomas à Kempis, *The Imitation of Christ*, bk. 1, chap. 3; and bk. 3, chap. 3.

16 Henry Suso.

17 See Kempis, *Imitation*, bk. 1, chap. 1.

18 Vain is the comfort afforded people of the world by the abundance of their earthly possessions; vain, too, their desolation over the loss of these goods. Bernard of Clairvaux, First Sermon on the Sixth Sunday after Pentecost.

To proffer you a worldly consolation would be neither pleasing nor becoming. Such consolation is empty and worthless and, what is most to be feared, it is even an obstacle to true and profitable consolation. Bernard, Fourth Sermon on the Vigil of the Nativity.

19 Henry Suso.

20 Says St. Augustine on the word *Paraclete*: "This Comforter or Advocate, (for the Greek word *Parakletos* will bear either interpretation) would be needful to them when they saw Christ no more." Ninth Lesson, Fouth Sunday after Easter.—Trans.

21 Cf. Thomas Aquinas, *Summa Theologiæ* [hereafter ST], I-II, q. 112, a. 5.—Trans.

22 Teresa, *Way of Perfection*, chap. 29.

23 In the Vulgate and in early Christian Latin, *refrigerare* and *refrigerium* frequently signify the refreshment and refection of a meal, of food and drink. Cf. 2 Tm 1:16; and Tertullian, *Apologeticum*, chap. 39.

24 Henry Suso.

25 Labor is the expenditure of one's strength, is personal exertion associated with burden, sacrifice, and, not infrequently, with pain. Heinrich Pesch, S. J.

26 "Comforter the Best, gracious Host, sweet Refreshment"—all this is the Holy Spirit in every need and woe of this transient earthly existence. This thought is expressed in the preceding verses. That the Holy Spirit, however, does not remove all care and misery from us here below but merely proffers refreshment, alleviation, and encouragement is pointed out by the little word *in* meaning "in," or "at," or "during."

Only in their heavenly home, those who die in the Lord "rest from their labors" (Apoc 14:13) and "neither shall the sun fall on them, nor any heat" (Apoc 7:16) and "God will wipe away all tears from their eyes" (Apoc 7:17).

27 Kempis, *Imitation*, bk. 2, chap. 10.

28 Ibid., bk. 3, chap. 54.

29 "We seek a holy, everlasting rest from labor and burden. This peace, however, consists not in sloth, but in unspeakable peace of joyful activity. Since this action of praising God takes place without exertion of the body, without fear and worry, there is no transition from rest to labor, that is, activity does not require the cessation of rest. No return to work and worry takes place, but we continue in an activity which is itself a component of rest; this labor is without burden. Good as well as evil souls love rest, but most souls do not know in what way they can attain this object. Only when the soul loves God does it find true, secure, and eternal peace which is sought in vain in other things.

"Since God sanctified the seventh day (the day of rest), the third commandment, which bids us keep holy the Sabbath day, directs our attention to the Holy Spirit, because from Him we receive the rest that we seek everywhere, but find only in the love of God, which 'is poured forth in our hearts through the Holy Spirit Who has been given to us' (Rom 5:5).

"All our good works we should perform with a view to obtaining this future eternal rest." Augustine, Letter 55 to Januarius.

30 Kempis, *Imitation*, bk. 1, chap. 25.

31 The movements and stirrings of the appetitive faculties, the so-called passions, promote the life of virtue insofar as they do not exceed the bounds of morality, serve a good purpose, and tend toward a moral good. Hence these affections are not to be suppressed, but to be tempered and directed into their proper channels.

32 Kempis, *Imitation*, bk. 3, chap. 55.

33 Ibid., bk. 2, chap. 10; and bk. 3, chap. 15.

34 Roman Breviary, Aug. 11.

35 Kempis, *Imitation*, bk. 3, chap. 16.

36 See Roman Missal.

37 Augustine, *Confessions*, bk. 4, chap. 5.

38 Consolatory Speech at Valentenian's Death.

39 Kempis, *Imitation*, bk. 3, chap. 34.

40 See Gregory the Great, *Pastoral Rule*.

41 Regrettable is the change made in the original exceedingly significant word *lumine: Sine tuo numine—nihil est in lumine* (without Thy Divinity, nothing shows up in its proper light), now changed to the weaker: *nihil est in homine*. P. Blume, S.J.

42 W. Weber.

43 To the point for preachers are the words of St. Ambrose: "If we cannot pronounce 'the Lord Jesus' without the Holy Spirit, then surely without Him we cannot presume to preach." *De Spiritu Sancto*, bk. 1, chap. 11, no. 124.—Trans.

44 See Roman Breviary.

45 Leo the Great, Sermon 1 on the Feast of Pentecost, chap. 2. See *Nicene and Post-Nicene Fathers*, series 2, vol. 12.

46 Leo the Great, Sermon 1 on the Pentecostal Fasts, chap. 3.

47 Kempis, *Imitation*, bk. 3, chap. 23.

48 Ibid., bk. 3, chap. 55.

49 Ibid., bk. 4, chap. 12.

50 Leo the Great, Sermon 1 on the Pentecostal Fasts, chap. 4.

51 Leo the Great, Sermon 4 on the Pentecostal Fasts, chap. 2.

52 Kempis, *Imitation*, bk. 3, chap. 5.

53 Ibid., bk. 1, chap. 11.

54 Leo XIII.

55 The sacred sevenfold gifts: wisdom, understanding, counsel, fortitude, knowledge, piety, and fear of the Lord (see Is 11:2–3).

56 The four-time recurrence of *give* harmonizes beautifully with the fourfold repetition of *come* in the first verse. Fervor and depth of longing for the glorious gifts, and for the gracious descent, of the Holy Spirit are expressed through this repetition of words.

57 The gifts of the Holy Spirit are not to be summarily dismissed as of little consequence in our spiritual life. And the reason? Simply because, as St. Thomas teaches (see ST, I-II, q. 68, a. 2), they are necessary to salvation, hence, must be assiduously cultivated by even the ordinary Christian. Highly to be recommended for enlightenment on this point is the perusal of the chapter "The Gifts of the Holy Ghost" in the book *The Spiritual Life*, by Very Rev. A. Tanquerey, S.S., D.D.—Trans.

58 **Who Does God's Work Will Get God's Pay**
Who does God's work will get God's pay,
However long may seem the day,
However weary be the way.

Though powers may thunder "Nay,"
No human hand God's hand may stay,
Who does God's work will get God's pay.

God hurries not, nor makes delay,
Who works for Him, will get His pay,
Some certain hour, some certain day.

He does not pay as others pay,
In gold or land or raiment gay,
In goods that perish and decay.

But God's high wisdom knows a way,
And this is sure, let come what may,
Who does God's work will get God's pay.
—Trans.

59 Roman Missal.

APPENDIX

VENI SANCTE SPIRITUS FORMAL EQUIVALENCE ENGLISH TRANSLATION

Veni, Sancte Spiritus, et emitte caelitus lucis tuae radium.	Come, Holy Spirit, and send out the heavenly ray of Your light.
Veni, pater pauperum, veni, dator munerum, veni, lumen cordium.	Come, father of the poor, come, giver of gifts, come, light of hearts.
Consolator optime, dulcis hospes animae, dulce refrigerium.	Greatest comforter, sweet guest of the soul, sweet consolation.
In labore requies, in aestu temperies, in fletu solatium.	In labor, rest, in heat, temperateness, in tears, solace.
O lux beatissima, reple cordis intima tuorum fidelium.	O most blessed light, fill the inmost heart of Your faithful.

Sine tuo numine, nihil est in homine, nihil est innoxium.	Without the nod of Your head, there is nothing in man, nothing that is harmless.
Lava quod est sordidum, riga quod est aridum, sana quod est saucium.	Cleanse what is unclean, water what is parched, heal what is wounded.
Flecte quod est rigidum, fove quod est frigidum, rege quod est devium.	Bend what is inflexible, warm what is chilled, correct what has gone astray.
Da tuis fidelibus, in te confidentibus, sacrum septenarium.	Give to Your faithful, who trust in You, the sevenfold gift.
Da virtutis meritum, da salutis exitum, da perenne gaudium. Amen.	Give of virtue's reward, give salvation's end, give joy eternal. Amen.

BENEDICTUS BOOKS

Our mission is to publish authentically Catholic books that are traditional, accessible, and beautiful.

Benedictus Books takes its name from the opening Latin phrase of the Canticle of Zechariah, prayed daily in the Catholic Church since the earliest centuries. Our logo evokes the antiquity of Gregorian chant and the illuminated manuscript tradition, emphasizing continuity with the faith and worship of the past and the continuing relevance of our sacred patrimony today.

Benedictus Books was established in 2021 with the launch of our acclaimed periodical *Benedictus*, the "Traditional Catholic Companion"—a daily devotional drawing on the theological riches and customs of the ancient Roman Rite, and allowing for a deeper experience of the traditional Latin Mass, liturgical calendar, and writings of countless saints and theologians. This periodical reflects the three core values of Benedictus Books:

Traditional. We are committed to preserving and handing on the Faith of our forefathers without diminution or change, publishing works that are both inspired by and conformable to traditional Catholic doctrine, liturgy, and spirituality. Our primary focus is on republishing reliably orthodox works that help to promote the interior life and sanctification of the domestic church through classical forms of prayer and worship.

Accessible. Recognizing that many aspects of Catholic doctrine, liturgy, and custom have become obscured in recent decades, we place an emphasis on texts that explain and assist readers in mining the vast theological wealth that is contained and expressed in the traditional Roman Rite, as well as those writings of saints and scholars that have been profoundly shaped by the same.

Beautiful. Rooted in the perennial tradition of Western sacred art, we believe that texts treating such exalted subjects deserve a truly beautiful and durable presentation. We invest extensive time and meticulous care to create inspiring new typesettings with rich ornament and illustration, crisp typography, clean layouts, and classic bindings to make every book as pleasing to hold and look at as it is to read.

In order to be worthy of the noble content they contain, all of our books are crafted to the most exacting standards, allowing these priceless treasures from our Catholic tradition to be cherished for years to come.